Scenic Driving
NEW MEXICO

Help Us Keep This Guide Up to Date

Every effort has been made by the author and editors to make this guide as accurate and useful as possible. However, many things can change after a guide is published—establishments close, phone numbers change, hiking trails are rerouted, facilities come under new management, etc.

We would love to hear from you concerning your experiences with this guide and how you feel it could be made better and be kept up to date. While we may not be able to respond to all comments and suggestions, we'll take them to heart and we'll also make certain to share them with the author. Please send your comments and suggestions to the following address:

The Globe Pequot Press
Reader Response/Editorial Department
P.O. Box 480
Guilford, CT 06437

Or you may e-mail us at:

editorial@GlobePequot.com

Thanks for your input, and happy travels!

Ⱥ**FALCON**GUIDE®

Scenic Driving
NEW MEXICO

Second Edition

LAURENCE PARENT

FALCONGUIDE®

GUILFORD, CONNECTICUT
HELENA, MONTANA

AN IMPRINT OF THE GLOBE PEQUOT PRESS

All photos by Laurence Parent
Maps by Tim Kissel © Morris Book Publishing, LLC

ISSN: 1553-2240
ISBN-13: 978-0-7627-3031-5
ISBN-10: 0-7627-3031-5

Manufactured in the United States of America
Second Edition/Second Printing

Contents

Acknowledgments

Numerous people helped me produce this book. I wish to thank my wife, Patricia, who accompanied me on my New Mexico travels when she could and took care of my office business when I was away. Thanks also to John Sanders and my father, Hiram Parent, who accompanied me on several trips.

David and Debbie Dozier, John and Emily Drabanski, Hiram and Annette Parent, Velva Price, Terry and Jonathon Hull, and Nancy Wizner all provided places to sleep, airport shuttles, and other essential favors during my travels. Many people of the National Park Service and the USDA Forest Service were very helpful with maps and information, particularly Ron Henderson and Bob Crisman.

Finally, thanks go to editors Randall Green and Elizabeth Taylor and The Globe Pequot Press for giving me another opportunity to visit New Mexico.

This book is dedicated to my parents,
who gave me my love of the outdoors.

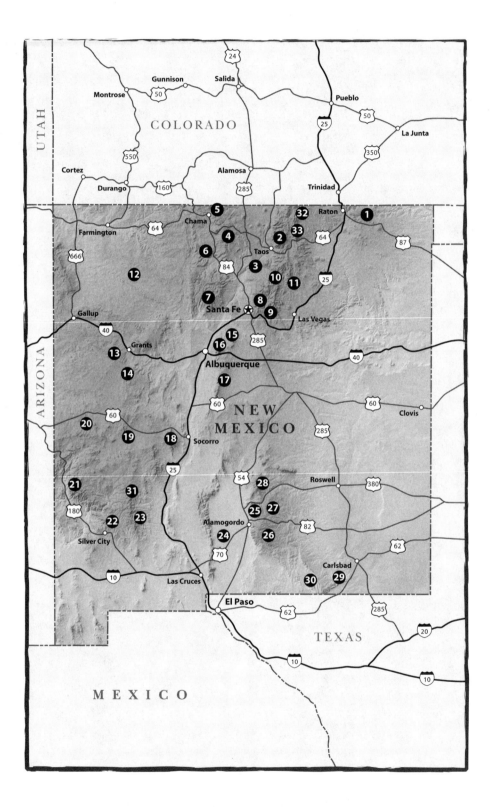

Map Legend

Interstate Highway/
Featured Interstate Highway

U.S. Highway/
Featured U.S. Highway

State Highway/
Featured State Highway

Paved Road/
Featured Paved Road

Unpaved Road/
Featured Unpaved Road

Railroad

Trail

Continental Divide

Visitor, Interpretive
Center

Headquarters

Campground

Building or Structure

Mine

Tunnel

Mountain, Peak, or Butte

Spring

River, Creek, or Drainage

Reservoir or Lake

State Line

National Park, National Forest,
Large State Park, or other
Federal Area

Wilderness Area

Small State Park, Wilderness
or Natural Area

Point of Interest

Ski Area

Amphitheater

Mission

Pass

▲ Pummel Peak
6,620 ft.

NEW MEXICO

Fall aspens on Sierra Blanca Peak, Lincoln National Forest (Drive 28)

Introduction

New Mexico is a land of contrasts, geologically and culturally. Alpine lakes repose in glacier-carved basins in the northern mountains, while wind sculpts white sand dunes in the south-central desert. Deep gorges of exposed basalts cut through the flanks of flat sandstone mesas, and mountain slopes covered by aspens and grassy meadows jut skyward only a few miles from dusty creosote plains.

Although New Mexico is the fifth largest state, it has one of the smallest populations, only about 1.9 million people. Most of the population lives in the Rio Grande and the lower Pecos River valleys. Only 3,500 people live in the 7,000 square miles of rugged Catron County, the state's largest, yet 600,000 crowd into much smaller Bernalillo County where Albuquerque lies.

The very old coexists with the very new. Archaeologists have found remnants here of some of the earliest known human cultures in the United States, such as Sandia and Folsom Man, yet the world's first nuclear bomb was exploded here. Thousand-year-old Indian ruins crumble into dust at Chaco Culture National Historical Park, and modern buildings reach for the sky in Albuquerque.

The land has been shaped by a multitude of geologic forces. Ancient seas have come and gone, depositing thick beds of limestones, shales, and sandstones. Vast reserves of mineral wealth—oil, gas, coal, and potash—lie within these beds, centered around Hobbs in the southeast and Farmington in the northwest. The ancient seas laid the groundwork for exceptional beauty, too. The decorated chambers of Carlsbad Cavern and other enormous caves are hidden within an ancient limestone reef near Carlsbad.

The uplift of the Rocky Mountains sculpted the rugged New Mexico landscape, creating dramatic peaks and valleys. Some mountains reach more than 13,000 feet high, while a long, narrow chunk of central New Mexico drops thousands of feet along a series of faults, creating the Rio Grande Rift. The Rio Grande River uses the rift as a path for its flow. Volcanoes erupted across the state, from the small cinder cone at Capulin Volcano National Monument to the vast 14-mile-diameter caldera at Valle Grande west of Los Alamos. These periods of folding, faulting, and volcanic activity also created enormous mineral wealth—gold, silver, copper, molybdenum, and other metals.

New Mexico has one of the highest average elevations in the United States. Elevations range from a low of 2,842 feet, where the Pecos River flows out of the state, to the high point, Wheeler Peak at 13,161 feet. Denver, Colorado, is famous as the Mile High City, but Albuquerque's altitude ranges from about 5,000 to 6,000 feet. Santa Fe, at 7,000 feet, is the highest state capital in the United States.

The broad elevation range of New Mexico provides a surprising variety of climates. The record high and low temperatures are an incredible 116 and minus 50 degrees Fahrenheit. Las Cruces, Carlsbad, and other southern desert cities have a mild climate attractive to sun lovers and retirees. These towns receive only a few short-lived snowstorms in the winter. Tucked up into the mountains, however, are ski towns such as Ruidoso and Red River that receive many feet of snow every year.

Many casual visitors to New Mexico picture the state as barren desert. Freeways such as Interstate 10 follow the easiest routes, often desert areas of flat, low-lying valleys; parts of the southern and northwestern deserts receive as little as seven inches of rain per year. However, air masses cool and expand as they rise over the New Mexico mountains and dump far more moisture, often thirty or forty inches of precipitation annually. Because the mountains are cooler and wetter, they support lush forests of pine, spruce, fir, and aspen. In fact, about a quarter of the state is wooded.

Much of New Mexico's charm is due to its mix of cultures. Until the Spanish explorer Coronado arrived in 1540, the Pueblo Indian culture of the upper Rio Grande Valley dominated the state. The arrival of the Spaniards led to a long period of Spanish, and then Mexican, domination. After the Mexican–American War ended in 1848, most of New Mexico was acquired by the United States. Anglos began arriving in large numbers along the Santa Fe Trail after the war ended. Today, the three cultures mix in an interesting blend, with its own unique food, architecture, art, and fashion.

Because New Mexico has some of the oldest roads in the United States, a book on scenic drives is particularly appropriate. The ancient Anasazi created an elaborate system of roads radiating outward from their villages in Chaco Canyon in northwestern New Mexico. Later, Spanish explorer Don Juan de Oñate established El Camino Real, the Royal Road, up the Rio Grande Valley from El Paso. It ultimately extended from Mexico City to Taos. One particularly notorious stretch came to be called La Jornada del Muerto (The Journey of Death or Dead Man's Route). The segment left the Rio Grande and crossed waterless desert where Indian attacks and thirst killed many travelers. Today, Interstate 25 follows much of the Royal Road.

The famous Santa Fe Trail brought considerable trade and commerce into northern New Mexico in the early and middle nineteenth century. The route was used heavily until a railroad was built over Raton Pass in 1879 and extended into Santa Fe.

New Mexico is blessed with vast amounts of public land. Most of the drives described in this guide pass through public land. The recreational activities along the roads are almost limitless—camping, hiking, bird-watching, hunting, fishing, skiing, boating, bicycling, rockhounding, and rock climbing. The towns along the way offer quaint restaurants, historic inns, and numerous art galleries.

Most of the drives in this guide follow paved roads. Some are broad highways, others are narrow and winding. A few dirt roads have been included, but all are usually well maintained and passable for most vehicles. However, a very few of the roads, mostly the unpaved ones, may be difficult to travel with large motor homes

Moreno Valley (Drive 11)

and trailers. The individual drive descriptions will give more details. A few of the high mountain roads close in winter, especially the unpaved ones.

Before setting out, be sure that your vehicle is in good condition. Top off your fuel tank, especially before driving some of the more remote highways. Check weather forecasts. Heavy snows can temporarily close even the main highways in winter. During the rainy season in late summer, the unpaved roads in this guide can get rough and occasionally even wash out. You may want to call the relevant agencies given in the "Helpful Organizations" appendix in the back for current road information.

Watch your speed. Some small towns, especially in northern New Mexico, have ridiculously low speed limits and are notorious speed traps.

Carry some extra food and water with you in case you have trouble on the road. Many of the drives pass through small towns and villages. Each drive description notes the availability of food, gas, and lodging, but realize the status can change with time. Don't count on finding gas stations and restaurants open late at night in small towns, where business hours tend to be longest in summer and shortest in winter.

The terrain these roads pass through is beautiful, but be sure to keep a close eye on the road. Watch out for blind curves and water crossings. Never drive into a flooded stream crossing. Most storms are short-lived and the water will quickly recede. Pull well off the road if you stop to sightsee. Watch out for deer and other animals on the road, especially at night. The author has had an unfortunate experience with a car and a mule deer. The incident was expensive to both. A few of these roads pass through open range, so also watch for livestock.

Please do your part to protect the scenic country you pass through. Be careful with fire, and be sure to thoroughly put out campfires and cigarettes. Stay on the designated roads; the land is fragile. Don't litter and don't disturb historic sites, such as ghost towns and Indian ruins.

Lastly, use the guide as an introduction. Follow that intriguing side road that disappears into the pines. Stop and stroll up a trail into a wilderness area. Hunt for fool's gold in an abandoned mine dump. Pull into a roadside cafe and try their blue corn enchiladas or green chile hamburgers. Take your time and discover the charm of New Mexico.

HOW TO USE THIS BOOK

Scenic Driving New Mexico describes thirty-three highway and backroad drives throughout the state. Each drive description is complemented with a map showing the route, campgrounds, special features such as historic sites, recreation areas, connecting roads, and nearby towns.

The descriptions are divided into the following categories.

General description provides a quick summary of the length, location, and scenic features of the drive.

Special attractions are prominent, interesting activities and features found along the route. Additional attractions are included in the description. Some activities, such as fishing and hunting, require permits or licenses that must be obtained locally.

Location gives the area of the state in which the drive is located.

Drive route number includes the specific highway names and numbers on which the drive travels.

Travel season notes if the specific route is open all year or closed seasonally. Some highways are closed to automobiles in winter due to snow but are open for snowshoeing, cross-country skiing, and snowmobiling. Opening and closing dates are approximate and subject to regional weather variations. Always check local conditions.

Camping includes listings of all state park, state forest, national forest, national park, and Bureau of Land Management campgrounds along the route.

Services lists communities with at least a restaurant, groceries, lodging, phone, and gasoline.

Nearby attractions are major attractions or activities found with 50 miles of the scenic drive.

The drive provides detailed traveler information, along with interesting regional history, geology, and natural history. Attractions are presented in the order a traveler encounters them when driving the route in the described direction. If you travel the route from the opposite direction, simply refer to the end of the drive descriptions first.

The **Helpful Organizations** appendix, at the end of the book, lists contact information for organizations that provide detailed information on the drive and its attractions.

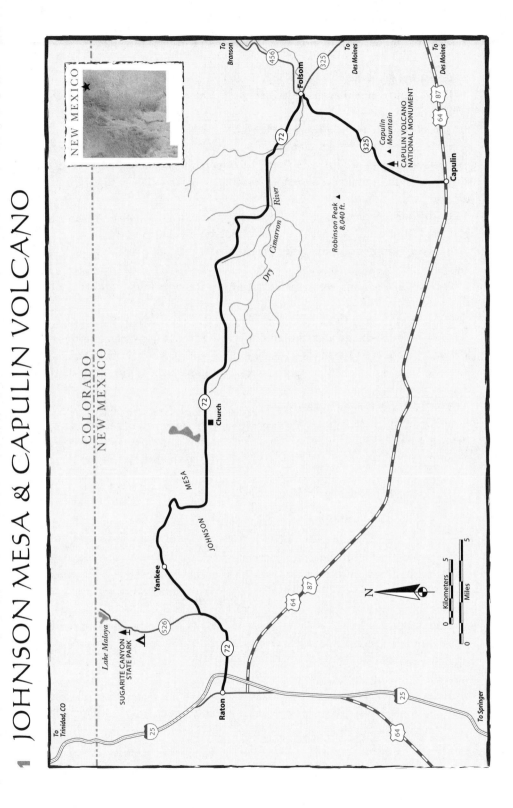

Johnson Mesa & Capulin Volcano

RATON TO CAPULIN

GENERAL DESCRIPTION: A 45-mile drive that follows the quiet back route from Raton to Capulin via Capulin Volcano National Monument.

SPECIAL ATTRACTIONS: Capulin Volcano National Monument, Sugarite Canyon State Park, Sugarite Ski Area, hiking, camping, views.

LOCATION: Northeastern New Mexico. The drive starts in Raton at the intersection of Interstate 25 and Highway 72.

DRIVE ROUTE NUMBER: Highway 72, Highway 325.

TRAVEL SEASON: Spring through fall. The drive is usually pleasant and cool in summer, with frequent afternoon rains. Snow can close the highway in winter.

CAMPING: Sugarite Canyon State Park.

SERVICES: All services are in Raton. Folsom has a restaurant with limited hours. Capulin has one gas station and food. Limited food and gas are in nearby Des Moines.

NEARBY ATTRACTIONS: Fort Union National Monument, Clayton Lake State Park, Sangre de Cristo Mountains, National Historic District in Trinidad, Colorado.

THE DRIVE

This drive follows the back road from Raton to Capulin. Thousands of cars zip through the two towns on busy U.S. Highway 64/87 on their way to Colorado or Texas, but very few travel Highway 72 and Highway 325. From **Raton,** the road climbs up through a broad canyon onto Johnson Mesa, a large, flat, grassy volcanic plateau. It then drops down into the Dry Cimarron River valley at Folsom. Extinct volcanoes, including Capulin Volcano, dot the grassy plains between Folsom and Capulin.

Late summer is an ideal time to make the trip. Most of the drive's elevation is more than 6,500 feet, and Johnson Mesa rises well over 8,000 feet, making for cool, pleasant weather. Summer rains turn the grasslands a lush, thick green. Dramatic storms boil up into the sky in the afternoons and dump showers across the region.

It may be difficult for large recreation vehicles (RVs) to negotiate the narrow highway as it winds through canyons and along the high mesa country. Some of the pavement is in poor condition, especially on Johnson Mesa, so allow plenty of time for the drive.

Sunflowers at Capulin Volcano National Monument

JOHNSON MESA

Follow Highway 72 east from Raton through a broad, grassy valley. After 2 miles, the highway turns northeast into the broad canyon of Chicorico Creek and passes a few scattered homes. At a little less than 4 miles, Highway 526 forks to the left. If you have time, be sure to take a short side trip up Highway 526, which follows the canyon's north fork and becomes narrower and steeper. A few abandoned coal mines and buildings dot the hillsides. The road crosses into **Sugarite Canyon State Park** in less than 2 miles, where two small lakes offer fishing. The upper one, Lake Maloya, is the larger. Ponderosa pine and Douglas fir become common on the slopes by the time the road reaches Lake Maloya. The park has trails around Lake Maloya and campgrounds. After about 6 miles, at the north end of Lake Maloya, the pavement ends and the road crosses into Colorado. Another small lake, Dorothey, lies in the Colorado State Wildlife Area just over the state line. A small local cross-country ski area, Sugarite, is located just a short distance up the road from Lake Maloya in Colorado.

Beyond the junctions with Highway 526, Highway 72 winds up the east fork of the canyon past a few homes in the village of Yankee. Soon the road climbs up and out of the canyon onto **Johnson Mesa.** In stark contrast with the steep, partly wooded slopes of the canyon, Johnson Mesa is a flat and nearly treeless plateau. Juniper and piñon pine inhabit the rocky escarpments along the north slope and ravines of the mesa. Thick grassland covers the mesa top. Only a few lonely ranches break up the stark terrain. Views open up of the Sangre de Cristo Mountains to the west and Colorado to the north. At one time, more people lived on the mesa. But most have left, driven out by drought and harsh winters. Here and there a few old barns and houses mark the sites of old homesteads. Along the highway in the middle of the mesa, a small church endures all alone. Once a year residents come to the church for the Sunday service and to relieve times past.

FOLSOM

After passing the church, several **volcanoes,** such as Capulin and Sierra Grande, become visible to the south and east. A few ponds lie in depressions on the mesa top. The road descends from the mesa top through groves of ponderosa pine, locust, and scrub oak into the valley of the Dry Cimarron River. A historic marker describes the site nearby where the first evidence was found of what became known as Folsom Man.

On August 27, 1908, a flood raged down the Dry Cimarron River from Johnson Mesa, killing seventeen people and destroying much of the town of Folsom. Many more would have died had not Sarah Rooke, the Folsom telephone operator, stayed at her switchboard calling people to warn them until the flood water swept her to her death.

The flood caused heavy erosion in the surrounding prairies and mountains, and George McJunkin, foreman of the Crowfoot Ranch, discovered large bones in the

Barn at Johnson Mesa

walls of a newly eroded arroyo. Scientists determined that some of the bones were from an extinct bison. In 1927 a spear point was found lodged in the earth between two bison ribs. Until then, most archaeologists believed that humans had only been in America for about 3,000 years. However, the bones in which the point was found were dated at about 9,000 to 10,000 years old, completely overturning earlier beliefs about human arrival in America.

In the village of Folsom, turn right at the junction with Highway 456. Drive through town and turn right again at the junction with Highway 325 and go toward Capulin. Be sure to stop at the **Folsom Museum** if you have time. Its hours are limited, especially during the winter. Folsom never really recovered from the devastating flood of 1908. It once was one of the largest cattle shipping points in the West but is now a quiet ranching center.

VOLCANIC AREA

South of Folsom, the highway crosses grassy plains dotted with volcanoes of the Raton–Clayton volcanic field. Over the course of several million years, numerous volcanoes erupted in northeastern New Mexico, spewing forth vast quantities of lava, cinders, and ash. Several of the volcanoes, including Capulin, Twin Mountain, and Baby Capulin, formed relatively recently, roughly 50,000 years ago. Folsom Man may well have witnessed some violent eruptions.

Be sure to stop in at **Capulin Volcano National Monument** to learn about the volcanoes. A narrow, paved road climbs to the summit of **Capulin Volcano.** A short loop trail circles the crater rim, giving spectacular views of craters dotting the grassy plains. On a clear day, views extend into Oklahoma, Texas, and Colorado.

From the monument, the drive continues about 3 miles south to its end at the junction with US 64/87 in the tiny community of **Capulin.** Capulin was the center of an area of dryland wheat and bean farming in the early part of the twentieth century. The drought-stricken Dust Bowl years of the 1930s forced the abandonment of most farms here. The fields have returned to prairie, and only a few widely scattered ranches remain.

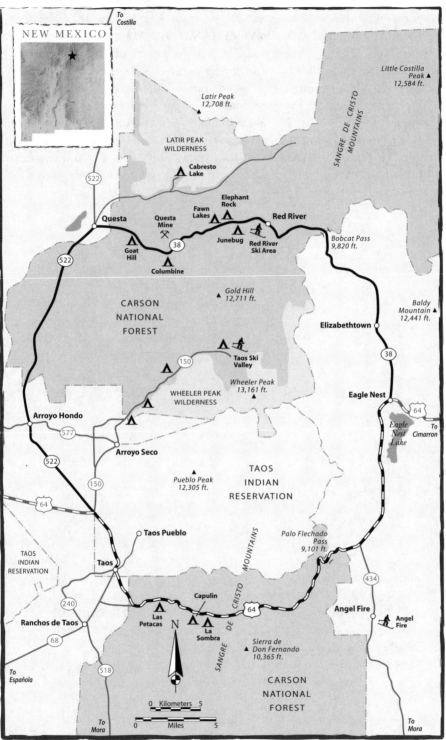

NEW MEXICO

To Costilla

Little Costilla Peak ▲ 12,584 ft.

Latir Peak 12,708 ft.

SANGRE DE CRISTO MOUNTAINS

LATIR PEAK WILDERNESS

Cabresto Lake

522

Elephant Rock

Fawn Lakes

Questa

Questa Mine

Red River

Junebug

Red River Ski Area

Bobcat Pass 9,820 ft.

Goat Hill

522

Columbine

CARSON NATIONAL FOREST

Gold Hill 12,711 ft.

Baldy Mountain ▲ 12,441 ft.

Elizabethtown

38

Taos Ski Valley

150

Wheeler Peak 13,161 ft. ▲

WHEELER PEAK WILDERNESS

Eagle Nest

64

Eagle Nest Lake

To Cimarron

Arroyo Hondo

577

Arroyo Seco

522

150

Pueblo Peak 12,305 ft.

TAOS INDIAN RESERVATION

64

Taos Pueblo

SANGRE DE CRISTO MOUNTAINS

Palo Flechado Pass 9,101 ft.

434

TAOS INDIAN RESERVATION

Taos

240

Capulin

Las Petacas

La Sombra

N

64

Angel Fire

Angel Fire

Ranchos de Taos

68

Sierra de Don Fernando 10,365 ft. ▲

To Española

518

CARSON NATIONAL FOREST

To Mora

0   Kilometers   5

0   Miles   5

To Mora

The Enchanted Circle

TAOS–RED RIVER LOOP

GENERAL DESCRIPTION: An 85-mile mountain loop circling the highest peak in New Mexico.

SPECIAL ATTRACTIONS: Historic Taos, Taos Pueblo, ghost town of Elizabethtown, Eagle Nest Lake, 13,000-foot peaks, Carson National Forest, Red River Ski Area, camping, hiking, cross-country skiing, fishing, scenic views, fall color.

LOCATION: North-central New Mexico. The drive begins in Taos and follows a loop east and north, beginning with U.S. Highway 64.

DRIVE ROUTE NUMBER: US 64, Highway 38, Highway 522.

TRAVEL SEASON: All year. Except for summer thunderstorms, the road is usually dry in spring, summer, and fall. The road can be icy and snowpacked in winter and early spring but is plowed regularly. Snow tires and chains may be necessary sometimes. The cool mountain temperatures make summer and fall drives ideal.

CAMPING: Multiple National Forest Service campgrounds lie east of Taos on US 64 and along Highway 38 west of Red River. Arrive early; they often fill up in summer, especially on weekends.

SERVICES: All services are available in Taos, Eagle Nest, Red River, and Questa.

NEARBY ATTRACTIONS: Taos and Angel Fire ski areas, Rio Grande Gorge, Cimarron River Canyon, Wheeler Peak Wilderness, Latir Peak Wilderness.

THE DRIVE

The Sangre de Cristo Mountains are New Mexico's highest, with summits reaching 13,000 feet and more. The range is part of the Rocky Mountains that extend south from Colorado into New Mexico. In Colorado the Sangre de Cristo Mountains become even higher, with several 14,000-foot peaks. This drive makes a loop around New Mexico's highest summit, 13,161-foot Wheeler Peak, by crossing two high mountain passes. The route passes lush forests, rushing streams, and cold mountain lakes, along with historic mining towns and a modern ski area.

The drive starts in **Taos,** the northernmost outpost of Spanish rule in the New World. Taos lay at the end of El Camino Real, or the Royal Road, the oldest European route in the United States. It stretched far down the Rio Grande Valley to El Paso and then onward to Chihuahua and Mexico City.

Taos Pueblo has been inhabited since about A.D. 1350, long before Columbus set foot in the Americas. The Spaniards discovered the pueblo in 1540 when one of Coronado's officers explored the region. In about 1617 a Spanish settlement was founded near the pueblo. Relations between the Indians and Spaniards were poor

San Francisco de Asis Church in Ranchos de Taos

and frequently violent. In 1680 the Pueblo Revolt of northern New Mexico forced the Spaniards to retreat down the Rio Grande Valley. Some years later, the Spaniards reestablished their settlement. After Mexico achieved independence from Spain, Taos fell under Mexican rule.

Anglo trappers began to drift into Taos after about 1820 to sell animal pelts and purchase supplies. After spending months trapping in the wilderness, their pursuit of alcohol and women upon arrival in Taos was legendary. After the Treaty of Guadalupe Hidalgo ceded most of New Mexico to the United States, Taos fell under American rule.

A combination of clear air, high elevation, sunlight, and the Spanish and Indian cultures began to attract artists to Taos early in the twentieth century. The artist colony continued to grow and is now famous. Shops and galleries line the old plaza and nearby streets. Droves of tourists flock in, especially in summer. If you tire of the crowds, head out on this scenic drive.

Unless you are going skiing, the drive is probably best done in summer or early fall. The route is beautiful in winter, but cold weather and deep snow limit outdoor activities along the way. This part of New Mexico is one of the most popular tourist centers in the state, so expect a fair amount of traffic, especially on summer weekends.

Taos lies on a flat 7,000-foot plain between the Rio Grande gorge on the west and the Sangre de Cristo Mountains on the east. Take US 64 east out of town toward Eagle Nest. The road quickly leaves the sagebrush-covered plateau by climbing up the canyon of the Rio Fernando de Taos. Ponderosa pines, Douglas firs, and aspens blanket the mountain slopes. Willows line the rushing mountain stream beside the road. Several national forest campgrounds and picnic areas lie along the creek. At the head of the river, the highway crosses the first pass, 9,101-foot Palo Flechado Pass.

EAGLE NEST LAKE

On the other side of the pass, the road makes a short, steep descent into the broad, open Moreno Valley. The small town of Eagle Nest lies in the center of the valley along the shores of **Eagle Nest Lake.** The high valley is surrounded by peaks on every side, including Wheeler Peak on the west side. The lake harbors large rainbow trout and even, surprisingly, kokanee salmon. The valley, at more than 8,000 feet, is one of the coldest spots in New Mexico. Fishermen cut holes in the ice of Eagle Nest Lake to fish in winter. On the south side of the valley, a few miles down Highway 434, skiers barrel down the slopes of Angel Fire Ski Area.

Before continuing north of Eagle Nest on Highway 38, consider driving a few miles farther east along US 64 into the **Cimarron River Canyon,** part of Drive 33. Below Eagle Nest Lake, the Cimarron River has cut a narrow outlet from the Moreno Valley through the mountains. The sheer canyon walls and rushing mountain river attract anglers and other outdoor enthusiasts.

North of Eagle Nest, Highway 38 climbs north up the valley. After about 5 miles, the road passes the remnants of **Elizabethtown.** In 1866 Ute Indians were trading native copper for other items at Fort Union. William Kroenig and W. H. Moore paid them to lead them to an ore body high on the slopes of 12,441-foot Baldy Mountain. During claim assessment work, gold was discovered. Word soon spread, and prospectors swarmed the mountain slopes. Many of the streams yielded placer gold and Elizabethtown developed rapidly. The small streams didn't have enough water to use dredging equipment, so a 42-mile-long ditch was built to transport water from the East Fork of the Red River. Lawsuits challenged the water diversion project, and water flow was below projections, so the ditch was eventually abandoned. Ultimately, most gold was removed from hard rock mines on the mountain slopes, rather than from streams. The ore finally played out, and fires and vandals destroyed most of the town. Today, little remains but crumbling stone walls, a few foundations, and a lonely cemetery.

RED RIVER AND QUESTA

North of Elizabethtown, Highway 38 climbs up over the 9,820-foot Bobcat Pass, the highest highway pass in New Mexico, before dropping steeply into the resort town of **Red River.** Like Elizabethtown, Red River is an old mining town. Ore discoveries were made in the hills above the town in the years after Elizabethtown was founded, but the mines were never particularly rich or fruitful. The town was named after the Red River, a mountain stream known for the red sediment carried by it after heavy rains. As the town's mining days faded, tourists from the hot flatlands of Texas and Oklahoma discovered the area as a summer escape. A downhill ski area built in the late 1950s turned the town into a busy year-round resort. Nearby, two wilderness areas, the Wheeler Peak Wilderness to the south and the Latir Peak Wilderness to the north, have many miles of scenic trails for hikers and horses. Mountain streams attract trout fishermen and old mining roads provide opportunities for back-road travel.

Highway 38 continues down the Red River Canyon to **Questa,** passing several national forest campgrounds along the way. High on the north canyon wall near Questa, massive scars mark a large molybdenum mine. Molybdenum, while not as glamorous as gold or silver, is an important ingredient in production of steel and other materials. The mine recently closed due to low molybdenum prices, but could reopen in the future.

Questa is a small town located at the mouth of the Red River Canyon. If you have time, be sure to visit the Rio Grande Gorge at the Rio Grande Wild and Scenic River a few miles west of town. The Rio Grande has carved an abrupt, 800-foot-deep canyon into the flat sagebrush plains at the base of the Sangre de Cristos.

From Questa follow Highway 522 south back to Taos. It follows a rolling route through the piñon-juniper–covered western foothills of the Sangre de Cristo Mountains. Views stretch for miles across the broad valley. Signs mark the turnoff to the ranch occupied by author D. H. Lawrence for a short period in the 1920s. Highway 522 rejoins US 64 just before Taos.

The High Road

SANTA FE TO TAOS

GENERAL DESCRIPTION: A 70-mile scenic back road from Santa Fe to Taos that passes through old Spanish villages and the foothills of the Sangre de Cristo Mountains.

SPECIAL ATTRACTIONS: Weavers in Chimayo, historic churches in Chimayo, Las Trampas, and Ranchos de Taos, Indian pueblos, Carson National Forest, Pecos Wilderness, Santa Fe, Taos, views, hiking, camping.

LOCATION: North-central New Mexico. The drive starts at the junction of Highway 503 about 15 miles north of Santa Fe on U.S. Highway 84/285.

DRIVE ROUTE NUMBER: Highway 503, Highway 520, Highway 76, Highway 75, Highway 518.

TRAVEL SEASON: Year-round. The highway can be snowy and icy in winter. Summer and fall are the most pleasant times.

CAMPING: Campgrounds are at Santa Cruz Lake, in the Carson National Forest, and in the mountains on side roads above Las Trampas and Peñasco and a few miles east of the scenic drive along Highway 518 on the highway to Mora.

SERVICES: All services are available in Santa Fe and Taos and nearby Española. Limited restaurants and gas are in Truchas, Peñasco, and Chimayo. Very limited lodging in Chimayo and Truchas.

NEARBY ATTRACTIONS: Bandelier National Monument, Santa Fe National Forest, Santa Fe and Sipapu ski areas, Rio Grande Gorge.

THE DRIVE

The fastest and most popular route between Santa Fe and Taos follows the Rio Grande Valley through Española. However, the High Road described here is more scenic and has a much smaller, although growing, volume of traffic. It's easy to take a full day for the drive, browsing in Chimayo shops, photographing the old churches, or hiking in the Pecos Wilderness. Speed limits on this route tend to be lower than the highway engineering allows, rarely exceeding 40 mph on the open road and 25 mph in towns. Local police use it as a revenue raiser, so watch your speed.

From **Santa Fe** go north on busy, four-lane US 84/285 about 15 miles to Pojoaque. Turn east on Highway 503 to Chimayo and Nambe Pueblo. For a few miles, the highway follows a small river valley with expensive homes tucked into cottonwood groves. The turnoff to Nambe Pueblo is on the right. It is one of several small Indian pueblos in the Española area. At Nambe, visitors can walk to a series of waterfalls on the Rio Nambe.

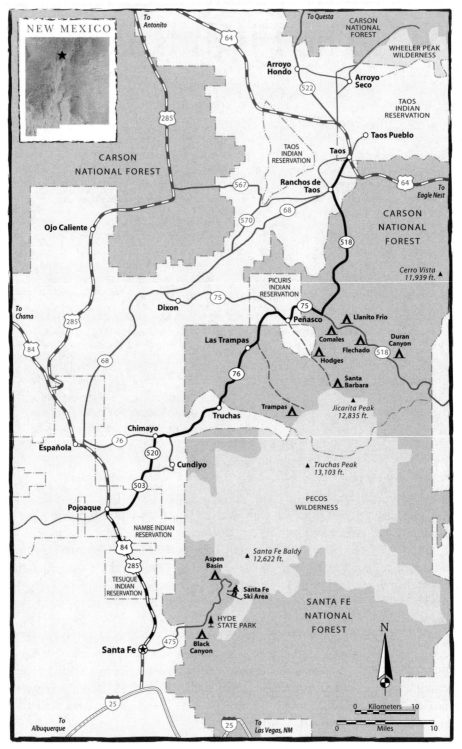

WEAVING AT CHIMAYO

The road soon climbs out onto dry, eroded hills dotted with juniper and piñon pine. In about 10 miles, the highway reaches **Chimayo,** a small village shaded by large cottonwoods. The old settlement, founded by the Spaniards, has long been known for its weavers. Early in the nineteenth century, residents of Santa Fe requested that Spain send over experienced weavers to teach the skills of the craft to the New World settlers. Two brothers, both skilled weavers, made the journey and settled in Chimayo and taught their craft there. Chimayo has been known for weaving ever since. Ortega's is one of the best-known shops where weavers have worked for many generations.

The village is also famous for its church, the Santuario de Chimayo, built by Don Bernardo Abeyta between 1813 and 1816. Legend tells that Abeyta was very ill when a vision led him to the site of the church, whereupon he was immediately cured. Filled with gratitude, he built the small sanctuary. To this day, pilgrims visit the church to collect small samples of sacred earth from a hole in the floor of a back room. Many believe that the dirt has curative powers.

Continue north through Chimayo to the junction with Highway 76. Turn right toward Truchas and Taos and begin climbing higher into the foothills. To take a side trip to Santa Cruz Lake, turn right on Highway 502 toward Cundiyo, after going

Santuario de Chimayo

only a couple of miles east of Chimayo. After another mile or two, turn right again on Highway 596 and follow signs to the lake. Highway 596 makes a short, steep, and winding descent to the small lake. The Bureau of Land Management operates the relatively little-known recreation area and provides campsites, fishing, and no-wake boating. The lake, tucked into a steep-walled valley of dry, eroded hills, is an unexpected sight. During the busy summer tourist season, try for a campsite here if other campgrounds are full.

Highway 76 climbs steadily to the village of **Truchas,** a small hamlet founded by the Spanish in the 1700s. Its hilltop setting provides spectacular views of the Rio Grande Valley to the west and the 13,000-foot Truchas Peaks to the east. Robert Redford selected the picturesque town for his movie *The Milagro Beanfield War.*

Highway 76 enters the **Carson National Forest** after Truchas and passes through thick ponderosa pine groves. The tiny settlement of Las Trampas was founded in 1751 by twelve Santa Fe families. The church that they built is a fine example of eighteenth-century architecture. Its outside choir loft and wooden bell towers are particularly notable.

These small Spanish-founded villages clinging to the slopes of the Sangre de Cristo Mountains are centers for the Penitente sect of the Roman Catholic Church. In the past, membership required penance of its initiates, including self-flagellation. After Archbishop Lamy learned of the practices, the church banned the Penitente societies in 1899. Their activities were driven underground until 1947, when the church again allowed Penitente practices, provided that the penances did no physical harm.

PECOS WILDERNESS

As you drive out of the north side of Las Trampas look below on the right for a flume carved from a single log. Just a little farther, Forest Road 207 provides a little-known but excellent access point to the **Pecos Wilderness.** Well-maintained hiking trails at the end of the road lead to the alpine Trampas and San Leonardo Lakes. The tiny lakes are sparkling jewels tucked in sheer-walled valleys carved by glaciers into the towering Truchas Peaks. A rustic campground is at the trailhead.

The highway passes through the village of Chamisal before dropping down into **Peñasco** at the junction of Highway 75. Turn right, or east, on Highway 75 and drive through Peñasco and then Vadito to the junction with Highway 518. While in Peñasco, you may want to take a side trip to the tiny Picuris Indian Pueblo. Another side trip, Highway 73 on the east end of Peñasco, leads to two Forest Service campgrounds—Santa Barbara and Hodges in Rio Santa Barbara Canyon. Several scenic Pecos Wilderness trails start from Santa Barbara Canyon. The aspens and cottonwoods here paint the hills with color during the fall.

At the junction of Highway 518 and Highway 75 go left on Highway 518 toward **Taos.** The highway climbs up through the Carson National Forest and over a low pass, U.S. Hill. A turnout at U.S. Hill provides good views of the forested

Autumn in the Carson National Forest

mountains. From the pass, the highway descends down a valley to the end of the drive at the junction with Highway 68. **Ranchos de Taos** is just to the left along Highway 68. Be sure to visit the old village, founded in about 1716. The church, built in the 1770s, was constructed of 4-foot-thick adobe walls with massive curving buttresses. Large wooden *vigas,* or beams, support the roof. The structure is probably one of the most photographed and painted churches in the United States.

The center of Taos lies 3.5 miles north along Highway 68. With its many art galleries, shops, restaurants, historic sites, and other attractions, it draws throngs of visitors daily.

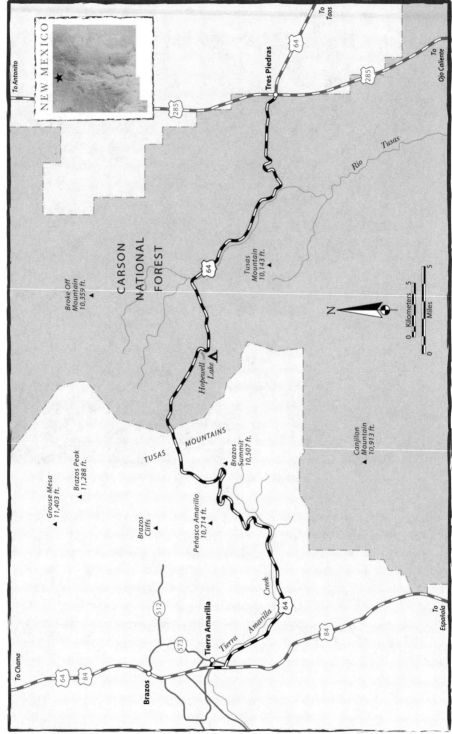

Brazos Summit

TRES PIEDRAS TO TIERRA AMARILLA

GENERAL DESCRIPTION: A 48-mile drive that climbs over the 10,507-foot Brazos Summit.

SPECIAL ATTRACTIONS: Brazos Cliffs, Hopewell Lake, Carson National Forest, aspens, scenic views, hiking, camping, fishing, cross-country skiing, cycling, mountain biking.

LOCATION: Northern New Mexico. The drive starts in Tres Piedras, about 30 miles northwest of Taos.

DRIVE ROUTE NUMBER: U.S. Highway 64.

TRAVEL SEASON: Late spring through fall. The route is usually dry in late spring, summer, and fall except for summer thunderstorms. The drive is cool and pleasant in summer. The road gets icy and snowpacked in winter. Snow tires and chains may be necessary. Highway crews plow the road in winter, but the road can close temporarily after heavy snows.

CAMPING: A national forest campground is maintained at Hopewell Lake.

SERVICES: Food and gas are in Tres Piedras, and gas is in Tierra Amarilla. The closest lodging is in Chama, 12 miles north of Tierra Amarilla.

NEARBY ATTRACTIONS: Rio Grande Gorge, Cruces Basin Wilderness, Cumbres and Toltec Scenic Railroad.

THE DRIVE

Between Tres Piedras and Tierra Amarilla, US 64 climbs up over a southern extension of the San Juan Range of the Rocky Mountains sometimes called the Tusas Mountains. The road reaches an elevation of 10,507 feet at Brazos Summit, making it the second highest point on a New Mexico highway. Along the way, it passes some of the most extensive groves of aspens in the state, making the drive ideal in late September and early October.

The drive starts in **Tres Piedras,** a small community at the western edge of the flat sagebrush plain that borders the Rio Grande Gorge. Many people will come from Taos for the drive. Those who do will cross the Rio Grande Gorge Bridge, a vertigo-inducing span suspended 600 feet above the river. When it was built in 1965, it was the second highest bridge in the world.

Tres Piedras is a small timber and ranching village that was settled in 1879. It was named for three rocky outcroppings of granite. The town lies at about 8,000 feet and is very cold in winter. Ponderosa pines are scattered around the town and become thick immediately to the west.

US 64 begins climbing gradually into the hills west of town and immediately enters the **Carson National Forest.** Unlike many of New Mexico's mountain roads, this highway is wide and has broad, easily negotiated curves. After about 6 or 7 miles, the highway drops a short distance into the valley of the Rio Tusas. A few scattered ranches and hay fields line the river. For the next 8 or 10 miles, the highway gradually climbs up the pastoral mountain valley.

The mountains here are relatively gentle and rolling as they climb toward the summit. Large meadows are interspersed with patches of pine, spruce, fir, and aspen. Forest Service roads turn off the main highway periodically, tempting one with possible side trips. Cross-country skiing is ideal here in winter.

The road eventually leaves the main river valley and climbs up a tributary to a minor summit before dropping down to tiny **Hopewell Lake.** A small, rustic national forest campground at the lake is popular with anglers and hunters. The lake is set in a grassy mountain valley lined with gentle wooded hills. An enterprising beaver has built a lodge at one end of the lake, using mud and aspen logs that he has gnawed down on the surrounding slopes and in part of the campground. The forest roads in the hills around the lake are not as steep and rugged as some in the New Mexico mountains and are ideal for casual mountain bikers.

BRAZOS SUMMIT AND CLIFFS

Beyond the lake, the highway resumes its steady climb. It drops one more time into a small valley at the Carson National Forest boundary. It then makes a final ascent to **Brazos Summit,** the high point of the drive. Spectacular views open up from pull-outs and picnic sites along the summit ridge. The western side of the mountain drops off much more abruptly than the eastern slope, allowing distant views to the west.

The rugged **Brazos Cliffs** tower into the sky a few miles northwest of the summit ridge. These towering cliffs of Precambrian quartzite were formed by faulting millions of years ago. During the peak of spring snowmelt or after heavy summer thunderstorms, a waterfall roars down the face of the cliffs. The cliffs are privately owned and should be viewed from the highway unless permission is obtained to enter. Two well-known resorts, Corkin's Lodge and Brazos Lodge, lie at the base of the cliffs along the banks of the Brazos River. They cater particularly to trout fishermen.

The highway descends quickly in big, swooping turns from the summit to the Chama River Valley. The western slopes of the mountain are blanketed with one of the best displays of aspens in the state. In fall the drive can be spectacular. Once the road leaves the steepest slopes, it descends gradually into **Tierra Amarilla** along Tierra Amarilla Creek.

The small town lies in the broad, pastoral Chama River Valley. It was founded in 1832 in the Tierra Amarilla Land Grant. Settlement was slow because of raids by Apaches, Utes, and Navajos. Because beaver were prolific in the area, it was origi-

Snow-covered Brazos Cliffs

nally named Las Nutrias. Later the name was changed to Tierra Amarilla, which means "yellow earth." It became the county seat of Rio Arriba County in 1880 but remains a sleepy mountain town with an economy based on grazing, timber, and tourism.

Unlike the busy highways near Santa Fe and Taos, this segment of US 64 has very little traffic. The wide highway, light traffic, and spectacular scenery also make the route ideal for cyclists.

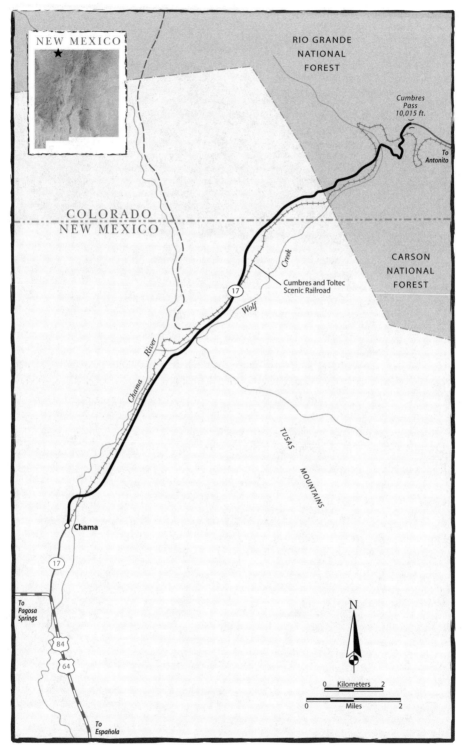

NEW MEXICO

RIO GRANDE
NATIONAL
FOREST

Cumbres
Pass
10,015 ft.

To
Antonito

COLORADO
NEW MEXICO

CARSON
NATIONAL
FOREST

Creek

Cumbres and Toltec
Scenic Railroad

17

Wolf

River

Chama

TUSAS

MOUNTAINS

Chama

17

To
Pagosa
Springs

84

64

N

0   Kilometers   2

0   Miles   2

To
Española

5

Cumbres Pass

CHAMA TO CUMBRES PASS

GENERAL DESCRIPTION: A 13-mile drive into the San Juan Mountains of Colorado along the route of the Cumbres and Toltec Scenic Railroad.

SPECIAL ATTRACTIONS: Cumbres and Toltec Scenic Railroad, Rio Grande National Forest, fall color, views, hiking, camping.

LOCATION: North-central New Mexico. The drive starts on the south side of Chama at the junction of Highway 17 and U.S. Highway 64/84.

DRIVE ROUTE NUMBER: Highway 17.

TRAVEL SEASON: All year. Summer and fall are the best seasons for the high-altitude drive. Expect ice and snow in winter and temporary road closures. Snow tires and chains often will be necessary.

CAMPING: Several campgrounds are managed by the Rio Grande National Forest at Trujillo Meadows Reservoir, near Cumbres Pass, and along the Conejos River in Colorado. A very pleasant private campground along the Chama River is on the north side of Chama, just north of the train station.

SERVICES: All services are available in Chama.

NEARBY ATTRACTIONS: Carson National Forest, Cruces Basin Wilderness, Chama River Wilderness, Heron Lake, El Vado Lake.

THE DRIVE

This drive is short but very scenic. It climbs through the San Juan Mountains of northern New Mexico and southern Colorado. The historic **Cumbres and Toltec Scenic Railroad** parallels the highway for much of the climb up to Cumbres Pass.

The drive starts on the south side of **Chama** and passes through the small town. The village began as a small sheep and cattle ranching community in the 1870s. With the discovery of rich gold and silver deposits in the San Juan Mountains of southwestern Colorado, the Denver and Rio Grande Railway began building tracks to connect the eastern plains with Durango, Silverton, and other mining camps. After much surveying, a route over 10,015-foot Cumbres Pass was selected for the route to Durango.

Because railroads were very difficult to build through the rugged mountains, narrow-gauge track was used to reduce costs. The width between rails with standard gauge is 4 feet, 8.5 inches, but the Denver and Rio Grande used a much narrower 3 feet. This allowed tighter curves, smaller tunnels and trestles, and a narrower roadbed.

21

A RAILROAD'S HISTORY

Construction of the railroad began with thousands of laborers blasting tunnels, building trestles, and laying track. The brutal work, combined with dreams of riches to be made in the mining boomtowns, led to high turnover among the workers. Chama boomed with the massive influx of construction people. Saloons and gambling dens bustled all night. Food and lodging were expensive, prices driven by the growing demand. Finally, early in 1881, the railroad arrived in Chama. A few months later, on July 27, the first construction train steamed into Durango.

The years between the arrival of the railroad and the Great Depression were Chama's glory days. Thousands of sheep grazed the mountain slopes. Sawmills cut lumber throughout the region. Trains rolled through constantly, feeding the mining towns to the west.

But the Depression brought hard times to the Chama River Valley. Many ranches failed, and loggers had decimated the forest. Trucks on newly paved roads were competing heavily for the railroad's freight traffic, and broad ownership of automobiles lessened the demand for passenger trains. The Denver and Rio Grande petitioned the Interstate Commerce Commission to abandon the line between Chama and Antonito in 1967. Area residents fought the abandonment, until finally the states of Colorado and New Mexico bought the historic track and equipment.

Today the narrow-gauge steam railroad carries thousands of people over Cumbres Pass to Antonito every year. The train clings to rails laid on the brink of Toltec Gorge and chugs through dark, smoky tunnels. Because so many people come to view the golden aspens that blanket the mountain slopes in fall, it is necessary to make reservations for the 64-mile train ride. The train runs from about Memorial Day weekend through fall color in mid-October. The railroad is also beginning to run a Christmas train in December. After more than one hundred years, Chama is still a railroad town.

If it is mealtime, stop in at Vera's restaurant for a hot plate of Mexican food or at the Elkhorn Café for good down-home American food before you begin the drive. The highway passes the railroad station and yards in the center of town. It is worth a stop to look at the old steam engines, even if you do not ride the train. You may want to time the drive to depart when one of the trains leave. Then you can watch the train from many vantage points along the road as it chugs by, belching thick black coal smoke. The highway climbs steadily northeast up the Chama River Valley into the aspen-covered slopes of the San Juan Mountains. The valley narrows and steepens as the road climbs, particularly after it leaves the Chama River. The highway crosses the Colorado state line and enters the Rio Grande National Forest shortly before reaching **Cumbres Pass.** At the pass, a small station and stopping point for the train offers another opportunity to view the historic steam engine and cars close-up.

Although the drive formally ends here, I highly recommend that you continue the additional 35 miles to Antonito on Colorado Highway 17. Beyond Cumbres

Cumbres and Toltec Scenic Railroad

Pass, the highway winds through several miles of lush mountain meadows to the slightly higher La Manga Pass. Along the way, the highway parts company with the railroad. The tracks descend to Antonito via Toltec Gorge and the Los Pinos River, while the highway drops down to the rushing Conejos River and follows it to Antonito.

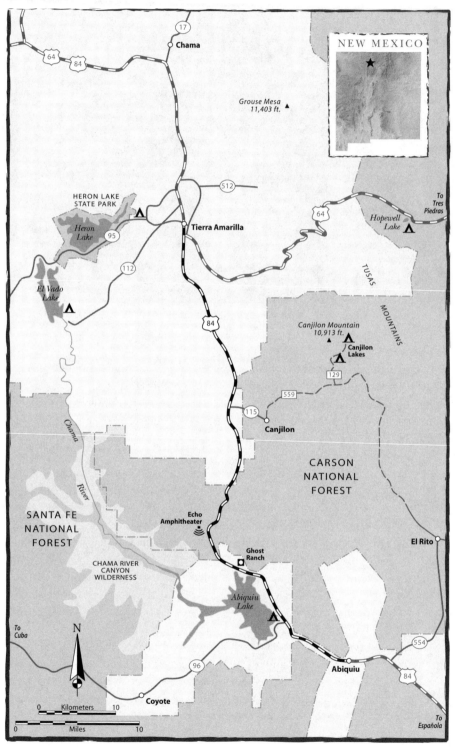

NEW MEXICO

17
Chama

64
84

Grouse Mesa
11,403 ft.

512

HERON LAKE
STATE PARK

Heron
Lake
95

64

Hopewell
Lake

To
Tres
Piedras

Tierra Amarilla

112

El Vado
Lake

84

TUSAS

MOUNTAINS

Canjilon Mountain
10,913 ft.

Canjilon
Lakes

129

559

115

Canjilon

Chama

River

SANTA FE
NATIONAL
FOREST

CHAMA RIVER
CANYON
WILDERNESS

Echo
Amphitheater

CARSON
NATIONAL
FOREST

El Rito

Ghost
Ranch

Abiquiu
Lake

To
Cuba

N

554

96

Abiquiu

84

Coyote

0   Kilometers   10

0   Miles   10

To
Española

Ghost Ranch

ABIQUIU TO TIERRA AMARILLA

GENERAL DESCRIPTION: A 45-mile drive through the red-rock country between Abiquiu and Tierra Amarilla.

SPECIAL ATTRACTIONS: Ghost Ranch, Echo Amphitheater, Abiquiu Reservoir, Carson National Forest, dinosaur fossils, camping, hiking, fishing.

LOCATION: North-central New Mexico. The drive starts in Abiquiu, about 22 miles north of Española.

DRIVE ROUTE NUMBER: U.S. Highway 84.

TRAVEL SEASON: Year-round. Fall is probably the most pleasant time of year for the drive. Winter storms will sometimes make the northern part of the route snowy and icy. At those times, chains and snow tires may be required.

CAMPING: An Army Corps of Engineers campground lies at Abiquiu Reservoir. The Carson National Forest maintains a campground at Echo Amphitheater and several in the mountains east of Canjilon, a village 3 miles east of US 84.

SERVICES: All services can be found in Española to the south of Abiquiu and Chama to the north of Tierra Amarilla. Limited food and gas can be found in Tierra Amarilla.

NEARBY ATTRACTIONS: Chama River Wilderness, Santa Fe National Forest, Heron Lake, El Vado Lake.

THE DRIVE

The drive starts in the cottonwood-lined Chama River Valley and slowly climbs north into the foothills of the Tusas Mountains, an extension of the San Juan Range of Colorado. Along the way, it passes some of the most scenic red-rock country in New Mexico and a graveyard of dinosaurs.

The route begins in **Abiquiu,** a small farming and ranching village that was settled in 1744 by a few Spaniards and Indian captives. Today, this sleepy village on the shady banks of the Chama River reveals little of its tumultuous and difficult beginnings. Making a living off the land was difficult because so little of it was arable. Ute Indian tribes from Colorado attacked regularly. A zealous priest found Abiquiu to be full of sorcery and sin, and a number of residents were even tried and convicted of witchcraft, similar to the trials in Salem, Massachusetts.

Abiquiu's most famous resident, painter Georgia O'Keeffe, lived for many years in the little village. She first came to New Mexico in 1930 and was enchanted by the terrain; the light in the clear, dry air; and the dramatic skies. O'Keeffe came every summer to live and paint at Ghost Ranch north of Abiquiu. She purchased and renovated an adobe house on a bluff overlooking the Chama River in 1945. The next year her husband died and she moved to Abiquiu permanently. She died

Chimney Rock at Ghost Ranch

in 1986 at age 98. Her softly textured paintings of the land around Abiquiu and Ghost Ranch have almost become trademarks of northern New Mexico.

A few miles north of Abiquiu, the valley narrows into a canyon, and the highway climbs out onto a mesa top. Abiquiu Reservoir is visible just to the west. Highway 96, which forks to the left, leads to the lake and crosses the dam. The lake level fluctuates greatly but still allows boating and fishing.

GHOST RANCH FOSSILS

The drive along US 84 continues north through mesas and buttes carved from thick beds of brick red, dusty yellow, and faded purple sandstone and shale. Gnarled junipers cling to the eroded slopes, eking out a difficult existence. A short distance off the highway lies **Ghost Ranch,** tucked into the base of Mesa Montosa. It was named for the *brujas,* or witches, that were supposed to haunt the mesas and canyons. The ranch was founded in 1766 but is now a convention and study center run by the Presbyterian Church. A number of movies have been filmed here, including the western *Silverado.*

The cliffs and hills of Ghost Ranch are not just colorful; they conceal the fossilized skeletons of dinosaurs. Many specimens have been found in the 250-million-year-old Triassic Period redbeds at the base of the sandstone cliffs. Particularly notable are remains of the coelophysis, one of the oldest known dinosaurs. The **Ruth Hall Museum of Paleontology** at the ranch displays and interprets some of the fossils. Next to the paleontology museum is the **Florence Hawley Ellis Museum of Anthropology.** It explains some of the human history of the area, from ancient times to the present.

A few miles north of Ghost Ranch, water has carved **Echo Amphitheater** into the Jurassic sandstone that forms the towering cliffs along the edge of the Chama River Valley. A short foot trail leads up into the huge stone alcove. Interpretive signs describe the geology and plant life. The smooth, curving walls produce almost perfect echoes from the slightest sound. The Forest Service maintains a picnic area and a campground at Echo Amphitheater.

North of Echo Amphitheater, the highway climbs up onto mesas and valleys that spill down from the Tusas Mountains to the east. Piñon pine and juniper dot the hills, along with scattered ponderosa pine. Cottonwoods, colorful in fall, line the creek bottoms. Time permitting, a worthy side trip leads east into the mountains above the village of Canjilon. Follow Highway 115 and the gravel Forest Roads 559 and 129 to **Canjilon Lakes.** The series of ponds and small lakes offer fishing and several campgrounds. The lakes lie at about 10,000 feet, so they are guaranteed to be cool even in summer.

The drive ends at **Tierra Amarilla,** a small village founded in 1832. The town's economy is based chiefly on agriculture. In 1967 the town gained fame as a center for disputes over land grant ownership. It climaxed with a shoot-out at the Rio Arriba County Courthouse, hostage-taking, and a massive manhunt for the activists in the nearby mountains.

7 VALLE GRANDE

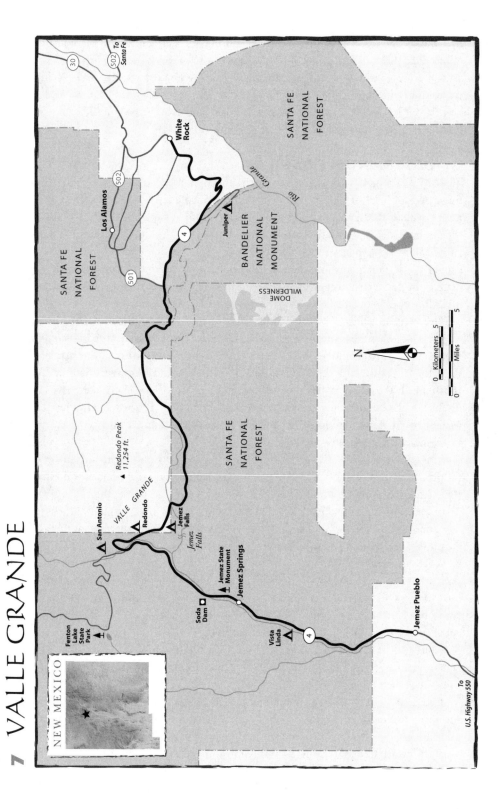

Valle Grande

WHITE ROCK TO JEMEZ PUEBLO

GENERAL DESCRIPTION: A 60-mile paved highway that winds through the Jemez Mountains, passing lush mountain meadows and ancient Indian ruins.

SPECIAL ATTRACTIONS: Bandelier National Monument, Valles Caldera National Preserve, Jemez Falls, Santa Fe National Forest, Jemez State Monument, Soda Dam, hot springs, hiking, cross-country skiing, camping, fishing, fall color.

LOCATION: North-central New Mexico. The drive starts in the town of White Rock, just a few miles southeast of Los Alamos.

DRIVE ROUTE NUMBER: Highway 4.

TRAVEL SEASON: Year-round. Summer and fall are the best times for this high-elevation route. Heavy snowfall can blanket the middle section of this drive, necessitating the use of chains and snow tires.

CAMPING: Bandelier National Monument has a campground. The Santa Fe National Forest maintains several campgrounds in the middle part of the route, Jemez Falls, Redondo, and San Antonio, and one between Jemez Pueblo and Jemez Springs, Vista Linda. Primitive camping is allowed throughout most of the national forest.

SERVICES: All services are available in Los Alamos and White Rock. Limited food and lodging are available in Jemez Springs. Gas is available on the highway between Jemez Pueblo and Jemez Springs and at the U.S. Highway 550/Highway 4 junction.

NEARBY ATTRACTIONS: Los Alamos, Santa Fe, Pajarito Ski Area, Fenton Lake State Park, and the San Pedro Parks Wilderness.

THE DRIVE

Highway 4 winds through miles of lush mountain forests as it crosses the Jemez Mountains. As with most mountain drives in New Mexico, it passes through several life zones, from scrubby piñon–juniper woodland to thick fir and aspen. Indian ruins, waterfalls, and hot springs add a special twist to this road.

The drive starts in **White Rock** on the Pajarito Plateau. White Rock is a relatively new town. It did not exist prior to World War II and has become a detached suburb of Los Alamos. Most White Rock residents work at the government labs in Los Alamos or in support businesses. Los Alamos itself developed only a few years before White Rock as a secret government laboratory for developing the atomic bomb. In the 1940s fences and guard towers circled the town, mail was censored, and travel was restricted. Although secret government research is still carried out at the labs, Los Alamos welcomes visitors today. The **Bradbury Science Museum** chronicles the development of the nuclear bomb and describes other scientific pursuits.

BANDELIER NATIONAL MONUMENT

From White Rock, Highway 4 goes west and crosses several interesting canyons that cut into the plateau. Most vegetation is piñon-juniper woodland, but some ponderosa grows in the canyons and other moist areas. Sadly, drought has killed much of the forest in recent years in this area. Bark beetles take advantage of droughts, killing many of the trees that the lack of moisture itself doesn't kill. The road forms the northern boundary of **Bandelier National Monument.** A short side road leads to the visitor center tucked in the bottom of Frijoles Canyon. A clear stream tumbles down the narrow canyon, shaded by a thick canopy of ponderosa pines and deciduous trees.

In the 1100s people settled Frijoles Canyon and other parts of the monument. They carved cave homes into the soft volcanic tuff of the canyon walls and constructed masonry dwellings on the canyon floors and mesa tops. Using rainfall and water from creeks, they cultivated corn, beans, and squash. For unknown reasons sometime in the early 1500s, the settlements were abandoned.

Today, hundreds of ruins are scattered up and down Frijoles Canyon and in other parts of the monument. Short, paved trails lead to many ruins near the visitor center. One particularly interesting ruin is at Ceremonial Cave. It requires a climb of 140 feet up a series of ladders, so it might not be a good choice for people with acrophobia. Another longer, but easy, hike goes down the canyon to two large waterfalls. Almost three-quarters of Bandelier is wilderness, so there are many opportunities for long day hikes and overnight trips.

Beyond the Bandelier turnoff, the highway climbs gradually northwest on the plateau. Ponderosa pines become dominant, although large areas of the forest were burned by the La Mesa Fire in 1977 and the catastrophic Cerro Grande Fire in 2000. The Cerro Grande Fire was started by the National Park Service as a prescribed burn. It quickly raged out of control and burned 50,000 acres, part of the city of Los Alamos, and part of the nuclear weapons laboratories. After the junction with Highway 501, Highway 4 begins climbing in earnest. As it winds up into the Jemez Mountains, tremendous views open up to the southeast. A thick forest of aspen and Douglas fir lines the road in unburned areas.

VALLES CALDERA NATIONAL PRESERVE

Shortly after leaving Bandelier National Monument, the highway drops into the broad mountain valley of Valle Grande. The valley is actually an enormous old volcanic crater, or caldera. The giant volcano exploded a million years ago with violent eruptions that dwarfed those of Mount St. Helens. Vast quantities of ash and lava spewed from the mountain. Without internal support, the volcano collapsed and formed a caldera 14 miles across. Geologists believe that the volcano was

Ceremonial Cave at Bandelier National Monument

between 15,000 and 25,000 feet tall before the collapse. The highest peak on the crater rim today is only 11,561 feet. The hardened and consolidated ash from the eruptions formed the canyon walls from which the first settlers of Bandelier carved their homes. Now, cattle and elk graze the grassy meadows of Valle Grande and thick forest cloaks the crater walls. In September and October, aspens add splotches of gold to the slopes. Although the mountains are tranquil now, magma still lies close to the surface, heating numerous springs. In 2000 the federal government acquired Valle Grande and set up a trust to manage it as **Valles Caldera National Preserve.** Limited access to the preserve is now possible via hiking trails along Highway 4 and with advance reservations.

The highway leaves the valley through a breach in the caldera wall carved by the East Fork of the Jemez River. Trout fishing is popular in the rushing waters of the river. To see **Jemez Falls,** take the short side road to Jemez Falls Campground. The large waterfall is a short walk from the campground.

Near Redondo Campground, a recreation site on the south side of the road has a short nature trail and a good overlook of the Jemez River Canyon. The road soon drops down into the canyon. The junction of Highway 126 lies in the canyon bottom. Highway 126 leads to many other beautiful areas of the Jemez Mountains, including the San Pedro Parks Wilderness, Fenton Lake State Park, and several campgrounds. After many miles, much of it on a gravel surface, Highway 126 ends in Cuba.

Beyond the junction with Highway 126, Highway 4 passes several picnic areas. At Battleship Rock, a trail climbs up to popular **McCauley Hot Spring.** The warm water is good for soaking any time of year. At one time someone stocked tropical fish in the pool, but it's doubtful any remain. The spring can also be reached by hiking down from Jemez Falls Campground. Numerous side trails branch off, so the trail can be confusing.

JEMEZ SPRINGS AND STATE MONUMENT

Mineral deposits from hot springs created the **Soda Dam** across a narrow spot in Jemez Canyon just upstream from Jemez Springs. As the hot water cooled, it precipitated calcium carbonate, or travertine, and built the dam. The river has cut a tunnel through the blockage.

Jemez Springs is a small settlement centered around hot springs in the canyon bottom. **Jemez State Monument** contains the ruins of the Giusewa Indian Pueblo and a fortress-like Spanish mission built in the early 1600s. The mission was abandoned in the 1650s, and religious activities moved to Jemez Pueblo at the mouth of the Jemez River Canyon. A short interpretive trail leads through the ruins, and a small visitor center features a number of exhibits.

From Jemez Springs, the highway gradually descends, following the river past towering red cliffs set off by tall, graceful cottonwoods that turn brilliant gold in fall. At the mouth of the canyon lies **Jemez Pueblo.** The adobe homes are grouped along a cluster of dusty streets. From shady *ramadas* along the highway, women sell bread baked in their outdoor ovens, or *hornos.* Be sure to stop and buy a loaf to mark the end of the drive.

Santa Fe Scenic Byway

SANTA FE TO SANTA FE SKI AREA

GENERAL DESCRIPTION: A dramatic 15-mile drive from the center of historic Santa Fe to the Santa Fe Ski Area tucked into a high valley of the Sangre de Cristo Mountains.

SPECIAL ATTRACTIONS: Santa Fe, Santa Fe Ski Area, Santa Fe National Forest, Pecos Wilderness, Hyde Memorial State Park, hiking, camping, fall color.

LOCATION: North-central New Mexico. The drive starts in Santa Fe.

DRIVE ROUTE NUMBER: Highway 475.

TRAVEL SEASON: Year-round. The drive is most pleasant in summer and fall. The road is plowed for skiers in winter. Chains or snow tires sometimes may be required.

CAMPING: The National Forest maintains Black Canyon, Big Tesuque, and Aspen Basin campgrounds along the route. All are small and tend to fill early in the day. Hyde Memorial State Park also has campsites. Primitive camping is allowed throughout much of the national forest.

SERVICES: All services are available in Santa Fe.

NEARBY ATTRACTIONS: Pecos National Historical Park, Bandelier National Monument, Jemez Mountains.

THE DRIVE

This national forest scenic byway is very popular because of its close proximity to Santa Fe. The drive starts at the old plaza in the center of town and climbs high into the lush forests of the Sangre de Cristo Mountains. Although Santa Fe has only about 50,000 residents, its fame stretches far and wide. A number of books have been written solely on the city. This brief description will serve only as an introduction.

Santa Fe was founded in 1610 by the Spaniards and is the oldest state capital in the United States. At an elevation of 7,000 feet in the foothills of the Sangre de Cristo Mountains, it is the highest state capital. The Palace of the Governors, built between 1610 and 1612, is the oldest government building in the United States. Artists have been attracted to Santa Fe and northern New Mexico for decades. Today, Santa Fe has one of largest numbers of art galleries in America. The city's adobe-style architecture gives Santa Fe a distinctive look.

Juan de Oñate arrived at a small Indian pueblo north of Santa Fe on July 11, 1598, with an expedition of settlers. They built a village called San Gabriel at the confluence of the Rio Grande and Chama Rivers. The settlement was not very successful, so a new capital was established in 1610 by Don Pedro de Peralta at the

SANTA FE SCENIC BYWAY

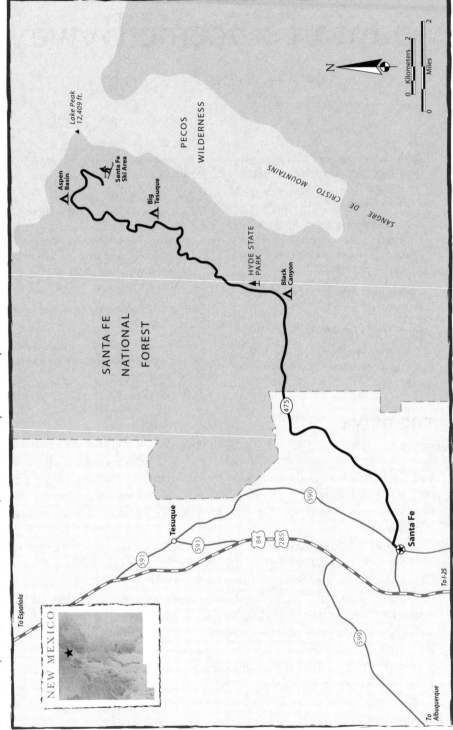

site of an abandoned Indian village. It was built along a mountain stream at the base of the Sangre de Cristo Mountains and christened La Villa Real de la Santa Fe. He constructed the Palace of the Governors, a walled fortress much larger then than it is today.

Spaniards settled the area around Santa Fe, but abuses by the settlers led to the Pueblo Revolt of 1680. Many were killed and the Spaniards were driven out and forced to retreat to El Paso. In 1692 Don Diego de Vargas retook Santa Fe after a bloodless standoff. The date, September 14, is still celebrated every year as the Santa Fe Fiesta.

AMERICA ENTERS SANTA FE

In 1821 Mexico gained its independence from Spain, and trade began with the United States along the Santa Fe Trail. The American presence increased steadily in Santa Fe. Finally, after the United States annexed Texas, the two countries went to war. By August 18, 1846, General Stephen Watts Kearny had marched into New Mexico and raised the American flag over the Palace of the Governors without firing a shot.

In 1862 Santa Fe was invaded yet again, this time by the Confederate Army during the Civil War. After a defeat in a battle at nearby Glorieta Pass, the Confederates abandoned Santa Fe. Their occupation lasted less than a month.

The railroad arrived in Santa Fe in 1880, accelerating settlement and growth in New Mexico. Statehood was applied for numerous times and finally granted in 1912. Almost 400 years after Santa Fe was established, it still is the center of state government.

Plan to spend several days in Santa Fe and the surrounding area. In summer try to make hotel reservations ahead of time. The town is swamped with tourists and rooms are scarce and expensive. Santa Fe has an incredible number of galleries, museums, historic buildings and churches, shops, and restaurants to occupy your time. When you tire of the city, head up the mountain on the scenic byway.

The drive starts in the Plaza downtown and can be a bit confusing at first. Work your way north of the Plaza, keeping an eye out for the ski area, Highway 475, and scenic byway signs. Eventually, the route climbs uphill through an expensive residential area toward the mountains. The forest soon turns from piñon and juniper to ponderosa. The road follows Little Tesuque Creek past Black Canyon Campground to **Hyde Memorial State Park.**

Above Hyde Park, the forest changes to Douglas fir, aspen, and other high-elevation trees. Views of the Rio Grande Valley open to the west. At night, the lights of Los Alamos are visible on the slopes of the Jemez Mountains. Several marked hiking trails start along the road. Big Tesuque Campground lies in the middle of a vast mountainside of aspens. Just a bit farther up the highway, Aspen Vista provides a broad view of the trees. A popular trail, actually a closed dirt road, starts at Aspen Vista and winds for several miles through the colorful trees. In early October, the

Inn at Loretto, Santa Fe

trees usually peak and cover the mountain with gold, making this drive one of the premier autumn spots in New Mexico. The aspens probably mark the site of an old forest fire that burned off the conifers.

SKIING SANTA FE

The highway ends a short distance farther at the **Santa Fe Ski Area.** The medium-size area attracts many downhill skiers on day trips from Santa Fe. The ski slopes look out over the Rio Grande Valley and beyond, providing spectacular views. The top of the ski area peaks at 12,000 feet, making it the highest in New Mexico and the second highest in the United States.

The Winsor trailhead lies at the base of the ski area parking lot by the tiny Aspen Basin Campground. The trail leads to popular destinations in the huge Pecos Wilderness. Hikers can pick from pristine alpine lakes (Nambe Lake and Lake Katherine), trout streams (the Rio Nambe), and high peaks (12,622-foot Santa Fe Baldy). After a good hike in the wilderness, drive back down Highway 475, relax with dinner in one of Santa Fe's 200 restaurants, and spend the evening at the famous outdoor Santa Fe Opera.

Pecos River

PECOS TO COWLES

GENERAL DESCRIPTION: A 19-mile drive from the town of Pecos to the headwaters of the Pecos River in the high Sangre de Cristo Mountains.

SPECIAL ATTRACTIONS: Pecos National Historical Park, Pecos Wilderness, Santa Fe National Forest, hiking, camping, fishing, fall color.

LOCATION: North-central New Mexico. The drive starts in Pecos, about 20 miles southeast of Santa Fe.

DRIVE ROUTE NUMBER: Highway 63.

TRAVEL SEASON: Late spring through fall. Snows usually close the upper part of the road in winter.

CAMPING: The Santa Fe National Forest and the New Mexico Department of Game and Fish manage several campgrounds along the route, with the highest concentration in the Cowles area. Primitive camping is allowed throughout most of the national forest.

SERVICES: All services are available in Pecos, although limited in quantity. A store is in Terrero. All services are available in nearby Santa Fe.

NEARBY ATTRACTIONS: Santa Fe, Santa Fe Ski Area, Villanueva State Park.

THE DRIVE

Highway 63 follows the Pecos River into the heart of the Sangre de Cristo Mountains, a southern extension of the Colorado Rockies. The drive starts in the historic village of Pecos and ends in high mountains forested with fir, aspen, pine, and spruce.

Pecos National Historical Park, about 2 miles south of Pecos, preserves and interprets the historical roots of the area. The hulking adobe ruins of the abandoned Spanish mission in the park mark the site of one of the most important pueblos in early New Mexico. Around A.D. 1100, Anasazi settlers from northwest New Mexico, along with existing groups, began to build centralized villages, or pueblos, in the Pecos River Valley. The pueblo at Pecos became the largest and most powerful. Trade between Pueblo and Plains Indians stimulated its growth. At its zenith, more than 600 rooms sheltered 2,000 residents in the four- or five-story structure.

The arrival of Coronado in 1540 changed the pueblo forever. When Coronado departed to search elsewhere for gold and riches, one priest stayed behind to attempt to Christianize the Indians. Several other Spaniards visited during the following years. After Oñate arrived in northern New Mexico in 1598, the Franciscans established a mission at Pecos to convert the Indians. A large church was built

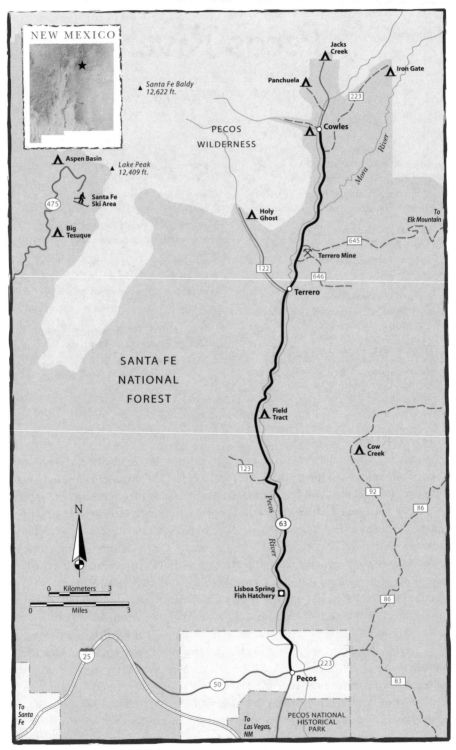

between 1617 and 1620. Drought, disease, famine, and suppression of the Indians' religious beliefs fomented the Pueblo Revolt of 1680. The Spaniards fled to El Paso and the mission was destroyed.

In 1692 the Spaniards returned, but the Pecos pueblo declined under new assaults. Comanche and Apache raids weakened the pueblo, and epidemics killed many residents. The Spaniards started another trading center down the river that hurt trade at Pecos. Finally, in 1838, the last seventeen survivors abandoned Pecos and moved to Jemez Pueblo. Beams of the church were removed and used in a corral in 1869. The adobe walls of what had been one of the largest and most important pueblos in New Mexico slowly crumbled and collapsed.

The modern village of Pecos was founded in about 1700. Its economy was closely tied to agriculture, but in the 1920s and 1930s the town experienced a boom when large mines up the Pecos River at Terrero were in operation. Just north of Pecos is the Benedictine Monastery, with its elaborate solar heating system. The New Mexico Department of Game and Fish oversees Monastery Lake just beyond the monastery. The small lake attracts trout fishermen.

As you drive north, the valley slowly narrows into a canyon and the forest becomes thicker. Here, the New Mexico Department of Game and Fish raises large numbers of rainbow trout at the **Lisboa Springs hatchery.** Visitors are welcome to view the operation.

A quaint adobe church sits by itself on the west side of the road about 8 miles north of Pecos, and several resorts line the Pecos River banks and cater to vacationers. The crystal-clear river rushes down the canyon, roaring over cascades and sliding silently through flat stretches while fishermen cast their lines under the shade of cottonwoods and willows that grow on the banks. At Terrero, which consists largely of a combined store and gas station, a narrow road forks left to Holy Ghost Campground. The campground lies along a rushing mountain stream at the end of the road. A popular Pecos Wilderness trailhead starts at the campground.

Terrero used to be a much larger town in the 1920s and 1930s when the mines were operating. Even a golf course was built across the wooded mountaintops. The mines, passed by the road a short distance up from the store, have long since been abandoned. The ore contained rich quantities of lead, along with other minerals. Unfortunately, some lead still remains in the mine tailings. Heavy rains sometimes leach it into the river, killing fish and creating other problems. The government, in an effort to solve the problem, disturbed some of the tailings and exposed more lead ore to weathering and the pollution worsened. You may see signs and fences marking the cleanup effort.

The road above Terrero is paved but is narrow, winding, and steep. Traffic can be heavy in summer, especially on weekends. Use care in traveling it.

The road passes the confluence of the Mora River, where the New Mexico Department of Game and Fish operates a rustic camp area and another Pecos Wilderness trail starts. A short distance past the Mora River, Forest Road 223 forks

Spanish mission church ruins, Pecos National Historical Park

right to Iron Gate Campground. The small campground lies in a thick forest of Douglas fir and aspen and is a popular Pecos Wilderness trailhead. However, the road to it is rough and suited only to high-clearance vehicles. After heavy rains it may be impassable.

The main road reaches **Cowles,** a small vacation home settlement, just beyond the Iron Gate turnoff. At Cowles, the main road ends. Three short spurs lead to campgrounds and trailheads at Panchuela, Jacks Creek, and Winsor Creek.

The 223,000-acre **Pecos Wilderness,** second largest in New Mexico, surrounds Cowles. The rugged headwaters of the Pecos River contained within the wilderness hold some of the most beautiful country in the state. Numerous sparkling lakes nestle in glacier-carved cirques at the foot of towering alpine peaks. The 13,000-foot Truchas Peaks, the second highest in New Mexico, preside over vast forests of ponderosa pine, Engelmann spruce, Douglas fir, aspen, and many other tree species. Above timberline, marmots and pikas search for food among wildflowers of the alpine tundra. Many miles of rushing trout streams tumble down rocky canyons to the Pecos River.

Thousands of hikers, backpackers, fishermen, horsemen, and hunters visit the wilderness every year. Many trailheads start along this drive, especially in the Cowles area. Be sure to at least take a stroll up one of the trails. Two of the easiest trails for a short hike follow Holy Ghost Creek and Panchuela Creek upstream from the campgrounds. Enjoy the cool, pine-scented air and the sound of bubbling mountain streams before starting your drive back to the city.

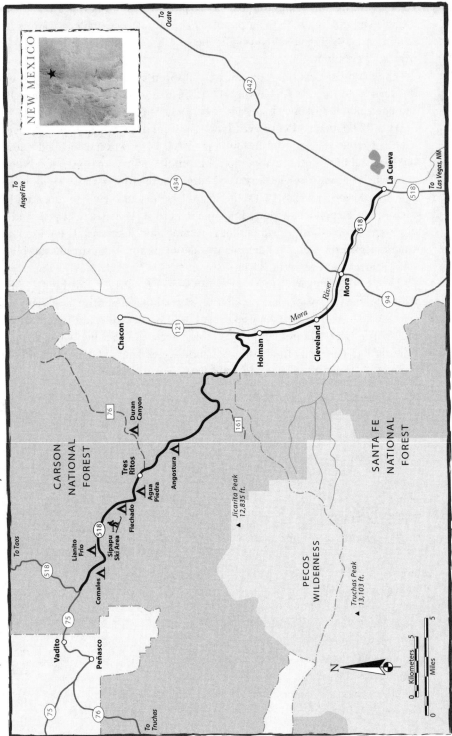

Sangre de Cristo Mountains & Mora Valley

VADITO TO LA CUEVA

GENERAL DESCRIPTION: A 33-mile drive over the heavily forested backbone of the Sangre de Cristo Mountains.

SPECIAL ATTRACTIONS: Pecos Wilderness, Carson National Forest, Salman Ranch, Cleveland Mill, Sipapu Ski Area, camping, hiking, fishing, fall color.

LOCATION: North-central New Mexico. The drive starts at the junction of Highway 518 and Highway 75 near Peñasco, about 20 miles south of Taos.

DRIVE ROUTE NUMBER: Highway 518.

TRAVEL SEASON: Year-round. Summer and fall are the best times for the high mountain

drive. Deep snow accumulates on the route in winter. The road is plowed, but chains or snow tires may sometimes be required.

CAMPING: The Carson National Forest manages several campgrounds along the highway and on side roads between the junction of Highway 518 and Highway 75 and the summit.

SERVICES: Mora has restaurants and gas. Sipapu Ski Area has gas, food, and lodging; Cleveland has limited lodging. Nearby Taos has all services.

NEARBY ATTRACTIONS: Fort Union National Monument, Taos.

THE DRIVE

The drive climbs over the Sangre de Cristo Mountains through lush forest, before dropping down into the pastoral Mora Valley. Much of the route follows a rushing mountain stream.

Start the trip at the junction of Highway 518 and Highway 75 south of Taos. The segment of Highway 518 between Taos and the junction is covered in Drive 3, the High Road. From the junction, Highway 518 climbs slowly southeast along the path of the Rio Pueblo. The rushing mountain stream has cut a rugged canyon through the mountains over the course of millennia. A dense forest of pine, fir, and aspen cloaks the mountainsides. The road passes national forest campgrounds at frequent intervals. Fishermen often are seen along this stretch, trying their luck in the clear, cold waters.

Hiker at Serpent Lake, Pecos Wilderness

Sipapu Ski Area is a small family-oriented ski area that attracts the same clients year after year. Their ski school is noted for its short-ski method of teaching. Unlike many large resorts, it has remained reasonably priced.

As the canyon climbs, it broadens until, near the summit, it opens up into a grassy valley. Aspens add color to the wooded slopes above in autumn. A number of marked hiking trails start from the highway along the canyon. Most climb up side canyons into the forest. Some of the trails going south lead into the vast **Pecos Wilderness.** Forest Road 161, a good gravel road, turns south off the main highway near the summit. It ends at a trail that leads to 12,835-foot Jicarita Peak, the Serpent Lakes, and many other spectacular destinations. Generally, this part of the Pecos Wilderness is much less crowded than areas around Santa Fe and Cowles.

After reaching the high point of the route, the highway drops rapidly down to the Mora River Valley. Several turnouts provide good views to the east. Once in the valley, the highway passes through a series of small villages.

CLEVELAND ROLLER MILL HISTORY

Be sure to stop at the **Cleveland Roller Mill Museum** in Cleveland. Until the mid-1800s, gristmills in northern New Mexico were small and primitive. By 1850, as the population grew, more farmers planted wheat in the area. The founding of Fort Union increased demand for flour even more. The St. Vrain Mill in Mora was the first large, efficient mill to be built in the area. Several others were constructed over the following years. In 1901 Joseph Fuss built the two-story Cleveland Roller Mill, the last one constructed in northern New Mexico. Fuss sold the mill to Daniel Cassidy, an Irish immigrant, in 1914. In the 1920s the mills in the Mora Valley reached their peak production.

Increasing industrialization and urbanization, along with the Depression, led to decreased wheat farming in the area. Between 1910 and 1980, the population of Mora County fell from 13,000 to 4,000 people. The Cleveland Mill was last used regularly in 1947. Intermittent use lasted for another seven years and then the mill fell into ruin. Beginning in 1984, a descendent of Daniel Cassidy began a painstaking restoration. After five years of labor, the mill was returned to its original condition. It is the only roller mill in New Mexico, if not the entire Southwest, to have its original milling works.

The water-powered mill is open to the public on weekends from Memorial Day through the end of October. Once a year, on Labor Day weekend, Cassidy opens the sluice gates and engages the water wheel, and the mill roars to life. Rubber belts hum, gears whir, wheels grind, and conveyors rise. The complicated maze of moving parts seems almost a parody of a nineteenth-century factory.

MORA AND LA CUEVA

The town of **Mora** was founded by Spanish settlers in about 1816. Lumber, agriculture, flour mills, and trade drove its economy. In its early years, Mora was not a

San Rafael Church, La Cueva

peaceful village. Comanche attacks were common, causing settlers to build their homes close together. The area also attracted its share of malcontents and criminals, leading to frequent feuds, murders, and lynchings.

La Cueva lies a few miles east of Mora along the Mora River. The small village was founded by Vicente Romero in the early 1800s. He tended sheep herds and, legend has it, slept in caves in the early years. After the Mora Land Grant of 1835, Romero acquired land from other grantees until he held 35,000 acres. He constructed a large irrigation system along the Mora River and grew grain, fruit, and vegetables. His large adobe home, built between 1835 and 1863, still stands today. High walls surrounded the house and corrals to protect them from Indian raids. A flour mill was built to grind wheat raised by the Romeros and other farmers. In its later years, the water-powered mill also generated electricity. The adobe San Rafael Church, with its Gothic windows, is being restored to its original 1860s condition. These and other buildings have been designated a National Historic District.

The Mora Valley was named for the wild raspberries that grew there. Today, the Salman Ranch in La Cueva raises raspberries commercially. To end your drive, stop in at the Salman Ranch Store and try a cup of ice cream with their homemade raspberry topping. A second cup will be hard to resist.

Angel Fire

MORA TO ANGEL FIRE

GENERAL DESCRIPTION: The 34-mile drive traverses a beautiful forested section of the Sangre de Cristo Mountains between the pastoral Mora River Valley and the ski resort of Angel Fire.

SPECIAL ATTRACTIONS: Coyote Creek State Park, Sangre de Cristo Mountains, Angel Fire ski area and resort, camping, fishing, fall color.

LOCATION: North-central New Mexico. The drive starts in Mora, a small town along Highway 518 between Las Vegas and Taos.

DRIVE ROUTE NUMBER: Highway 434.

TRAVEL SEASON: The best season is summer and fall, with pleasantly cool, high-elevation weather. Afternoon thunderstorms are common in late summer. Heavy snows fall in these mountains and can close the road temporarily in winter.

CAMPING: Coyote Creek State Park has campsites.

SERVICES: All services are available in Angel Fire. Gas and food can be obtained in Mora. Cabins are available just north of Coyote Creek State Park.

NEARBY ATTRACTIONS: Taos, Cleveland Roller Mill Museum, Pecos Wilderness, Carson National Forest, Fort Union National Monument.

THE DRIVE

The drive not only passes through the lush, grassy valleys and forested slopes of the **Sangre de Cristo Mountains** but it also passes through time. It starts in Mora, a small Hispanic town settled in about 1816, and ends in Angel Fire, a modern resort town with skiing, golf, and other outdoor activities. Unlike most of the drives in New Mexico, this one passes largely through private land. Please respect the rights of property owners.

Between Coyote Creek State Park and the junction with Highway 120, Highway 434 is steep and winding. Part of the drive does not have a full two lanes or a center line and may not be suitable for large recreation vehicles and trailers.

Highway 434 turns north from Highway 518 in the center of the small business district of Mora. For the first few miles, it crosses the lush Mora Valley. Modest homes and small farms dot the valley floor. Tall cottonwoods line the Mora River and irrigation ditches. The highway then climbs over a low divide forested with ponderosa pines into another lush valley dotted with widely scattered farms and ranches. A tiny tin-roofed adobe church is on the right side of the road in the middle of the valley.

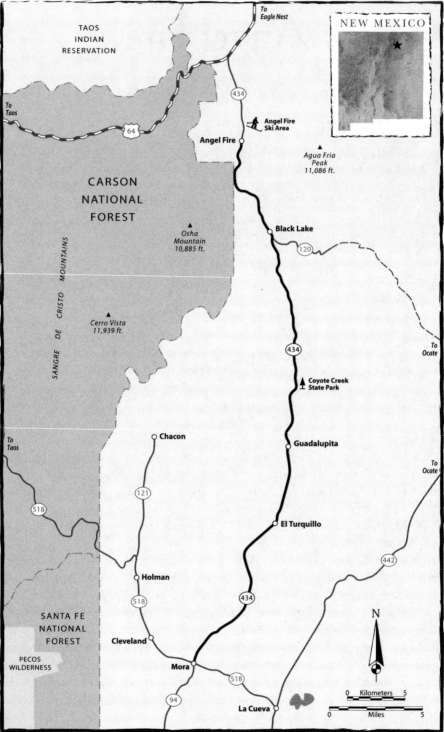

To Eagle Nest

TAOS INDIAN RESERVATION

NEW MEXICO

To Taos

64

434

Angel Fire Ski Area

Angel Fire

Agua Fria Peak 11,086 ft.

CARSON NATIONAL FOREST

Osha Mountain 10,885 ft.

Black Lake

120

SANGRE DE CRISTO MOUNTAINS

Cerro Vista 11,939 ft.

434

To Ocate

Coyote Creek State Park

To Taos

Chacon

Guadalupita

To Ocate

121

518

El Turquillo

442

Holman

518

434

N

SANTA FE NATIONAL FOREST

PECOS WILDERNESS

Cleveland

Mora

518

0 Kilometers 5

94

La Cueva

0 Miles 5

Horses on a frosty morning, Sangre de Cristo Mountains

The highway enters the valley created by Coyote Creek at the tiny village of Guadalupita. The town was more substantial at the turn of the twentieth century when farming, ranching, and logging fueled its economy. Beyond Guadalupita, the valley narrows and the road begins to climb more steeply. The small **Coyote Creek State Park** offers camping, picnicking, hiking, and fishing a little north of Guadalupita. Just beyond the state park is a full-service RV park and some rental cabins. The road narrows after the state park.

From the state park, the highway follows Coyote Creek, a clear, rushing mountain stream lined with blue spruce and Douglas fir, up to a pass, the divide between the Moreno Valley and the Coyote Creek watershed. The road gradually descends into the upper Moreno Valley, a broad open swath of lush mountain meadow with marshes and two small lakes, the Black Lakes. To the north, across the meadows, tower snowcapped peaks centered around 13,161-foot Wheeler Peak.

After passing a small group of vacation homes, the road intersects Highway 120. Beyond the junction, Highway 434 has been reconstructed into a broad highway with wide shoulders. The highway slowly descends through the Moreno Valley and begins to encounter outlying housing developments of Angel Fire near small Monte Verde Lake.

The drive ends in **Angel Fire.** The community started in the mid-1970s as a ski area, which is visible on the mountain slopes east of the highway. Initially the resort had some problems, but it has since developed into a bustling year-round resort with downhill and cross-country skiing, golf, hiking, fishing, and many other outdoor activities. The ski area is now one of the largest in the state. From Angel Fire, Highway 434 continues 3 miles to its end at U.S. Highway 64, another scenic drive described in this guide, the Enchanted Circle.

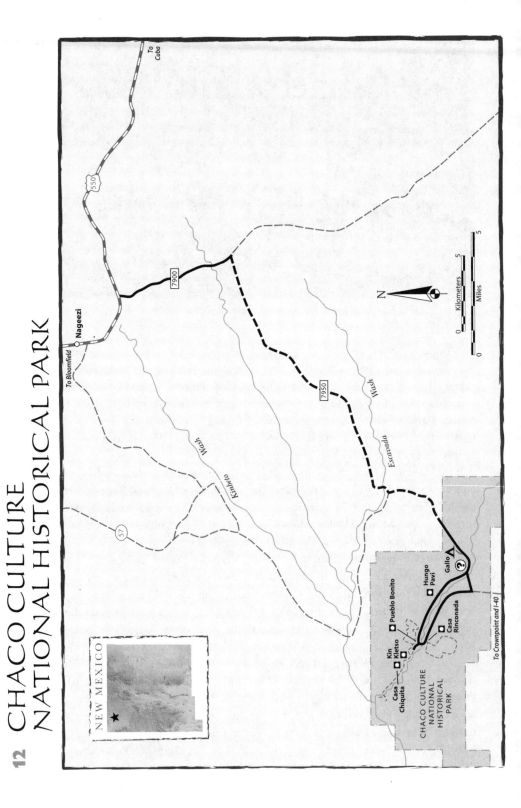

Chaco Culture National Historical Park

U.S. HIGHWAY 550 TO CHACO CULTURE NATIONAL HISTORICAL PARK

GENERAL DESCRIPTION: A 30-mile paved and dirt road to the ruins of one of the largest centers of Anasazi civilization in the United States.

SPECIAL ATTRACTIONS: Chaco Culture National Historical Park, Anasazi ruins, hiking, mountain biking, camping.

LOCATION: Northwestern New Mexico. The drive starts near mile marker 112 about 40 miles southeast of Bloomfield and 48 miles northwest of Cuba on U.S. Highway 550 at the junction with County Road 7900. The junction is marked with signs for Chaco Culture National Historical Park.

DRIVE ROUTE NAME/NUMBER: County Roads 7900 and 7950, Chaco Culture National Historical Park roads.

TRAVEL SEASON: All year. Spring and fall are

the most pleasant times. The drive can be hot in summer and cold in winter. Part of the route is dirt and can be muddy and slippery after rains or occasional winter snows. If weather is or has been bad, call (505) 786–7014, extension 221, before coming.

CAMPING: There is a campground at Chaco Culture National Historical Park.

SERVICES: All services can be obtained in Farmington, Bloomfield, and Aztec. Some food can usually be obtained at convenience stores along US 550.

NEARBY ATTRACTIONS: Aztec Ruins National Monument, Salmon Ruins, Shiprock, Angel Peak Recreation Area, Navajo Lake State Park, El Malpais National Monument, El Morro National Monument, Bisti/De-Na-Zin Wilderness, Navajo Reservation.

THE DRIVE

A thousand years ago, Chaco Canyon was the political and economic center for a large area of northwestern New Mexico. The residents built impressive stone pueblos that were interconnected with an extensive system of roads. Ruins dot the area today, especially within the park.

The drive starts at the junction of US 550 and CR 7900 40 miles southeast of Bloomfield at mile 112.5. The junction is marked with signs for **Chaco Culture National Historical Park.** Turn south from US 550 on paved CR 7900. The pavement ends after about 5 miles at the junction with CR 7950. Turn right on CR 7950, a broad dirt road notorious for its washboard surface. Road conditions vary considerably depending on rainfall, snow, and the most recent grading. Except when it's wet, the road is usually passable by any vehicle. The old north route into the park, Highway 57, has been closed at the park boundary and cannot be used.

The land rolls gently, with low mesas and broad valleys. The climate is dry; except for widely scattered piñons and junipers, the land is treeless. You'll pass a few homes, but the country is very lightly inhabited. The surrounding area contains a mix of Bureau of Land Management, Navajo, and private land. The region has a very remote, wide-open feel.

CHACO CANYON

About 21 miles from US 550, the road enters the park and becomes paved. It drops down into **Chaco Canyon,** passes the campground on the right, and quickly arrives at the visitor center. The center describes the history of the park ruins and has artifact exhibits, interpretive books for sale, water, and restrooms. Be sure to stop in for a park entrance permit, plus free permits required for walking any of the park's hiking trails.

Masonry pueblos, such as those at Chaco, were begun in the A.D. 700s. By the late 900s, large, elaborate, multistory pueblos known as great houses were being built in Chaco. A system of roads connected the large pueblos of Chaco Canyon with outlying settlements in the Four Corners area. A new masonry technique was developed that allowed walls to be built several stories high. Workers constructed two parallel walls with shaped sandstone rocks chinked with smaller stones and mortar. They filled the space between the two walls with mortar and rubble.

In the mid-1100s, the Chaco culture began to decline, possibly because of a long period of drought combined with depletion of local natural resources. The people migrated to Southwestern pueblos at Zuni, Acoma, Hopi, and the upper Rio Grande Valley. Warfare and cannibalism may have hastened Chaco's demise. By the end of the thirteenth century, the massive stone pueblos of Chaco Canyon were abandoned.

RUINS TO VISIT

A short trail leads from the visitor center to **Una Vida,** a partially excavated ruin discovered, along with the rest of Chaco Canyon, by Lieutenant James Simpson in 1849. Petroglyphs decorate the cliff walls above the ruin.

The paved, one-way, 9-mile loop drive starts at the visitor center. It is open from sunrise to sunset. A bicycle makes a great way to tour the loop road. The road first hits Hungo Pavi, a large, unexcavated great house with more than 150 rooms. The next stop is the parking area for Chetro Ketl and Pueblo Bonito. Chetro Ketl requires an easy 0.5-mile walk to and around the second largest ruin in the canyon.

Pueblo Bonito is the largest and most complex ruin in Chaco Canyon. It was built in stages and ultimately contained about 600 rooms and rose at least four sto-

Chaco Culture National Historical Park

ries high. The D-shaped structure occupied three acres and was centered around a plaza with about forty kivas. Large amounts of wood were used to build roofs, floors, and door lintels. There are few trees around Chaco Canyon today, possibly because the inhabitants of these pueblos cut them down for firewood and building materials.

In about another mile the road reaches **Pueblo del Arroyo,** another large pueblo ruin. Two of the park's main trails begin here. Be sure to obtain a hiking permit before doing them. The trails share a route, the old park entrance road, to an impressive multistory ruin, Kin Kletso, a short distance from Pueblo del Arroyo. From Kin Kletso, one trail continues west down the canyon on the old road to Casa Chiquita and the large Peñasco Blanco ruin. Along the way you pass numerous petroglyphs, historic markings, and, on a short spur, the famous Supernova pictograph. The round-trip distance is 6.4 miles, so take water, a hat, and sunscreen. In summer start early in the day. The other trail, the Pueblo Alto Trail, climbs up to the canyon rim from Kin Kletso through a cleft in the rock. It splits into a loop trail and goes to two ruins on the mesa top, an ancient stairway, and excellent overlooks of the canyon and several ruins. This hike is 5.4 miles round-trip, so go prepared.

A short distance beyond Pueblo del Arroyo on the loop road lies **Casa Rinconada** on the right. The ruin contains one of the largest kivas in the Southwest.

The structures, usually built at least partly underground, probably served as sites for religious ceremonies, communal gatherings, and other activities. Another back-country trail starts here, to Tsin Kletzin ruin. After Casa Rinconada, the loop returns to the visitor center.

If you only have time for one hike, take the Pueblo Alto Trail from Pueblo del Arroyo. It offers a great view of Pueblo Bonito from the cliff above. The path reaches the mesa top at Pueblo Alto. Miles and miles of empty country are visible in every direction. Few trees break up the monotony of the desert grasslands and mountains that lie far in the distance. The lonesome wind whistles through the walls and rubble of Pueblo Alto. Only ruins remain from the thousands of people that once lived in and around Chaco Canyon.

13

El Malpais & El Morro National Monuments

GRANTS TO EL MORRO

GENERAL DESCRIPTION: A 43-mile paved highway past the lava flows and volcanoes of El Malpais National Monument to the inscriptions of El Morro National Monument.

SPECIAL ATTRACTIONS: El Malpais National Monument, El Morro National Monument, Cibola National Forest, New Mexico Mining Museum, ice caves, hiking, camping.

LOCATION: Northwest New Mexico. The drive starts in Grants at the junction of Highway 53 and Interstate 40.

DRIVE ROUTE NUMBER: Highway 53.

TRAVEL SEASON: Year-round. Spring and fall are usually the most pleasant times. Afternoon thunderstorms frequently break the daytime heat in late summer, making it a pleasant time of year, as well. Winters can be cold. Occasional snowstorms can make driving hazardous, but the roads are dry most of the time.

CAMPING: El Morro National Monument manages a small campground. The Cibola National Forest operates three campgrounds in the Zuni Mountains to the north and west of the drive. Primitive camping is also allowed in most of the national forest.

SERVICES: All services are available in Grants.

NEARBY ATTRACTIONS: Chaco Culture National Historical Park, Mount Taylor, Bluewater Lake State Park, Acoma Pueblo.

THE DRIVE

Much of this drive follows the edge of a strange landscape, the lava flow known as the Malpais, or "bad land." Only a few thousand years ago, the most recent eruptions of a string of volcanoes south and west of Grants poured out vast flows of lava onto the broad valley south of I–40. The lava cooled into a wrinkled, twisted landscape of black rock. Lava tubes snake along under the surface; where they have collapsed, they leave deep trenches across the landscape. The lava, filled with air pockets, is a good insulator. In places, the tubes are deep enough to contain ice year-round. Jagged edges and deep cracks make the lava flow difficult to cross. Gnarled ponderosa pines and alligator junipers eke out an existence in pockets of soil. In areas where pines grow thickly, it is easy to become lost. In 1987 Congress designated El Malpais a national monument.

55

13 EL MALPAIS & EL MORRO NATIONAL MONUMENTS

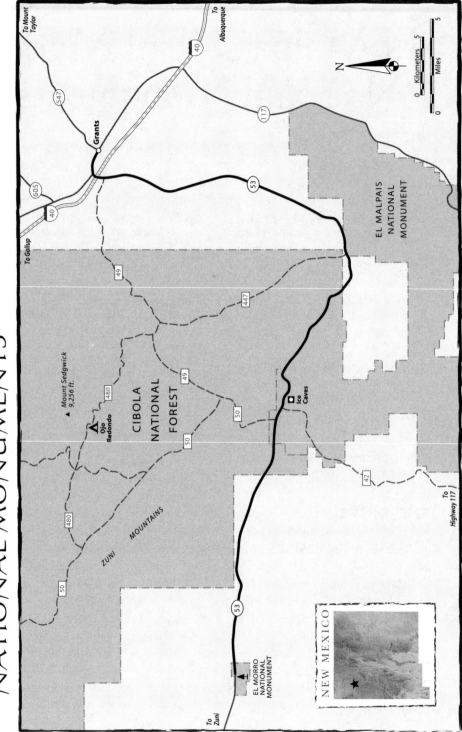

The drive starts in **Grants** at the north end of the Malpais. To the northeast, Mount Taylor looms over the town. The 11,301-foot volcano erupted for a period of two million years, beginning about four million years ago. The large volume of ash, cinders, and lava surrounding the peak suggests that Mount Taylor destroyed itself several times, only to rebuild again.

Since its founding in about 1872, the town of Grants seems to perennially be in a period of boom or bust. The first boom began in 1881 with the coming of construction crews for what became the Santa Fe Railroad. The 4,000 construction workers turned the sleepy settlement into a rowdy, bustling town. Logging in the Zuni Mountains contributed heavily to the area's economy until the mountains were stripped of trees. By the 1920s the population had dwindled to a few hundred. When Bluewater Lake was built, irrigation created an agricultural boom in growing carrots. This, too, tapered off in the 1940s. Then in 1950 Paddy Martinez, a Navajo sheepherder, found uranium ore west of Grants and set off another boom. Prospectors discovered some of the largest uranium deposits in the United States around the town. Martinez staked a claim, but the Santa Fe Railroad owned the land. However, the railroad paid him a reward for his discovery. With it, he moved to a simple Navajo hogan by Bluewater Lake and resumed grazing sheep.

By 1960 Grants' population had rocketed past 10,000. In 1981 Grants became the county seat of Cibola County, the first county created in New Mexico in thirty-two years. But the boom faded soon after. Some mines were depleted of ore, but most closed when uranium prices collapsed. Today, the mines are closed, some permanently, others until prices recover. The mining museum in town has created a simulated underground mine and other exhibits to chronicle the area's mining history.

EL MALPAIS NATIONAL MONUMENT

A few miles south of Grants, Highway 53 follows a narrow strip of land between the lava flows and the Zuni Mountains, passing through the small village of San Rafael. A large spring helped spur the settlement of the community. About 16 miles south of Grants, look for the marked trailhead for the Zuni-Acoma Trail. The ancient trail crosses the lava flow within **El Malpais National Monument** and was used for many centuries as a travel route between the Acoma and Zuni pueblos.

After the trailhead, the road turns west and begins to climb toward the Continental Divide. Ponderosa pines become more common. The highway continues to climb into a wooded cluster of cinder cones. Lava flows at the base of the volcanoes seem as jagged and bare as the day they poured out of the craters and vents. A short side road goes to the **Ice Caves** and **Bandera Crater.** For a small fee, the steep-walled crater and frigid ice caves can be visited. As of this writing, the caves and crater are privately owned, but the National Park Service plans to purchase the area eventually for El Malpais National Monument.

Inscription Rock, El Morro National Monument

Just beyond the Ice Caves turnoff, the highway crosses the Continental Divide and gradually descends to the west. All drainages on the east side of the divide eventually end up in the Atlantic Ocean, while all western drainages flow to the Pacific.

El Morro, at the end of the drive, marks the site of many historic inscriptions. A natural basin of fresh water at the base of the 200-foot-high bluff attracted travelers for many hundreds of years. First the Anasazi carved petroglyphs into the soft, yellow sandstone. Later the Spaniards left many inscriptions. Oñate, the leader of the first Spanish settlers in New Mexico, left his mark: PASSED BY HERE THE GOVERNOR DON JUAN DE OÑATE, FROM THE DISCOVERY OF THE SEA OF THE SOUTH ON THE 16TH OF APRIL, 1605. The Gulf of California was the Sea of the South. Many other Spaniards carved their names and messages, followed by Americans after the mid-1800s. Not surprisingly, the bluff is called **Inscription Rock.**

A short hiking trail visits the carvings at the base of the bluff and then climbs up onto the top. Two Anasazi pueblos occupy easily defended positions on the crest of the sheer-walled bluff. The two small villages were settled in about 1275. Dryland farming, hunting, and gathering sustained the pueblos until they were abandoned about 75 years later.

Find a ponderosa pine on top of the bluff and relax in its cool shade. The view sprawls out in all directions. The wooded Zuni Mountains lift up to the north. Sandstone mesas rise from sagebrush-covered valleys. Enjoy the tranquillity before returning to Grants or continuing on to Ramah and other villages of the Zuni Indian Reservation to the west.

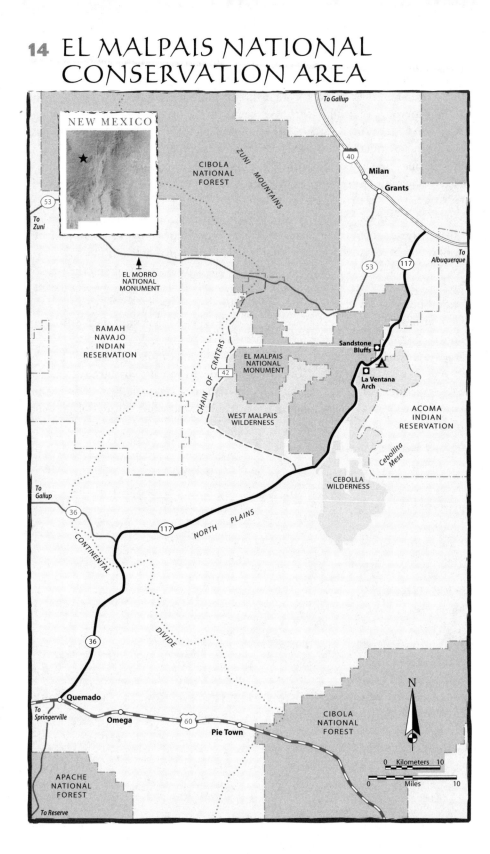

El Malpais National Conservation Area

GRANTS TO QUEMADO

GENERAL DESCRIPTION: A 78-mile paved highway through sandstone bluffs, natural arches, lava flows, and high plains.

SPECIAL ATTRACTIONS: El Malpais National Monument, El Malpais National Conservation Area, La Ventana Arch, Cebolla Wilderness, Continental Divide, hiking, camping.

LOCATION: Northwest New Mexico. The drive starts about 5 miles east of Grants at the junction of Interstate 40 and Highway 117.

DRIVE ROUTE NUMBER: Highway 117, Highway 36.

TRAVEL SEASON: Year-round. Late spring through fall is the best time to visit. Early summer can be quite hot, but afternoon thunderstorms often break the heat in late summer. Winters can be very cold, especially in Quemado. Occasional snows can make the highway treacherous, but most of the time the road is dry.

CAMPING: Primitive car camping is allowed at the Narrows. As of this writing, the Bureau of Land Management is building a campground along Highway 117 just south of the Sandstone Bluffs. The Narrows campground will close upon its completion. The Cibola National Forest maintains a campground northeast of Grants on the road up Mount Taylor.

SERVICES: All services are available in Grants. Quemado has limited food, gas, and lodging.

NEARBY ATTRACTIONS: Acoma Pueblo, Quemado Lake, Mount Taylor, El Morro National Monument.

THE DRIVE

Highways 117 and 36 between I–40 and Quemado traverse one of the least populated sections of New Mexico. Once you leave I–40, the traffic dries up and the rugged land and vast sky dominate. Tall sandstone cliffs, jagged lava flows, and high grassland alternate along the route.

Highway 117 follows a narrow corridor between lava flows to the west and Cebollita Mesa and Mesa Negra to the east. The route passes through segments of **El Malpais National Monument** and **El Malpais National Conservation Area.** The areas were so designated to recognize and protect the unique terrain.

The vast lava flows that fill the valley were created by a series of eruptions from volcanoes and vents along the south and west sides of the valley. The most recent

Sandstone Bluffs pool at El Malpais National Monument

flow occurred within the last few thousand years. Because road construction is difficult and expensive across lava, the highway stays just to the east of the flow. East of the road, the dusty yellow sandstone cliffs of Cebollita Mesa and Mesa Negra rise into the sky. About 9 miles south of I–40, the Bureau of Land Management has a ranger station on the left.

Just beyond the ranger station, a good gravel road turns off to the right to the **Sandstone Bluffs.** The short side road climbs up to an overlook, possibly the most scenic spot on this drive. The view from the top of the sandstone cliffs encompasses much of the vast lava flow called El Malpais, or "bad land." The Spanish named it well. The black surface is riven and splintered. Jagged chunks of sharp-edged rock point skyward. Deep trenches cross the flow, marking collapsed lava tubes. Travel across the flow is difficult at best.

Across the flow to the west rise the Zuni Mountains, and to the north towers Mount Taylor, an 11,301-foot extinct volcano. Junipers, gnarled and bent by the ceaseless wind and harsh, dry conditions, grow on the tops of the bluffs. A few ponderosa pines cling to pockets in the cliffs below the overlook, fed by water runoff from above. Try to visit the bluffs at sunset. The slanting sunlight paints the cliffs golden yellow as the lava flow falls into deep shadow. The last rays of sun turn Mount Taylor pink before fading into twilight.

A few miles south of the Sandstone Bluffs, the National Park Service has marked one end of the **Zuni-Acoma Trail** on the west side of the road. The old trail, one of the few places to cross the lava flow, is part of a historic route connecting the Zuni and Acoma pueblos. To get a feel of the lava flow, walk a short distance on the marked trail.

LA VENTANA

A little beyond the Zuni-Acoma trailhead, the Bureau of Land Management has built a parking area and short trail to **La Ventana,** the second largest natural arch in New Mexico. Water carved the massive sandstone span from the cliffs of Cebollita Mesa. Although the arch is tucked into an alcove, it can be seen clearly from the parking lot. The trail to the arch is short, but steep. It leads under the arch to the back of the alcove.

Beyond La Ventana, the highway enters the Narrows, so named because the lava flowed right up to the base of the mesa cliffs, leaving a very narrow corridor for the road. Old, twisted ponderosa pines grow from cracks in the lava. A small dirt side loop turns left off the highway at the south end of the Narrows and rejoins the highway in a half mile. Primitive camping and picnicking are allowed here.

After the Narrows, several broad canyons open up in Cebollita Mesa on the east side of the highway. Unimproved dirt roads, suitable for four-wheel drive, lead into the canyons. The roads cut through the **Cebolla Wilderness,** a 62,000-acre tract protected by the Bureau of Land Management that lies between Highway 117 and the Acoma Indian Reservation. The elevation of the wilderness ranges from 6,900 feet at the highway to 8,300 feet on top of the mesa. Piñon-juniper forest dominates, but ponderosa pine and some Douglas fir are not uncommon in moister areas such as drainages and north-facing slopes.

After the Narrows, the corridor between the mesa and the lava flow broadens. In about 10 miles, the highway leaves the last of the lava flow behind and crosses the North Plains. The high-elevation grasslands are almost devoid of human habitation. Lone windmills pump water for grazing cattle. Traffic is usually light to nonexistent. The view stretches for miles to the ragged peaks of the Sawtooth Mountains far to the south, and the sky seems infinite.

Eventually the highway climbs gradually to the intersection with Highway 36 in some piñon-juniper–covered hills. Turn left, south, on Highway 36 to Quemado. In 2 or 3 miles, the highway crosses the **Continental Divide,** the dividing line between the Atlantic and Pacific watersheds. The last few miles of Highway 36 descend into the village of **Quemado,** the end of the drive.

QUEMADO

Quemado means "burnt" in Spanish. Several stories explain the origin of the name. One says that the Apaches had burned much of the sagebrush around the town. Another tells of an Apache chief who burned himself in a campfire. Yet another claims that the name came from some burned-looking volcanoes in the area.

Quemado lies on the Magdalena Livestock Driveway, or Beefsteak Trail. It was a long route that stretched from eastern Arizona to the railhead in Magdalena. Enormous herds of cattle and sheep were driven over the trail to market from 1885 to the 1950s. Amazingly, the last segment of the trail did not close until 1971, making it the last regularly used cattle trail in the United States.

Today, Quemado is a small town catering to travelers, local ranchers and other area residents, and hunters in season. As tiny as it is, Quemado is one of the few towns in Catron County. The county is New Mexico's largest but least densely populated county, with about 2.5 square miles per person.

The Turquoise Trail

TIJERAS TO SANTA FE

GENERAL DESCRIPTION: A 48-mile paved highway that passes through several historic towns and the foothills of the Sandia, Ortiz, and San Pedro Mountains.

SPECIAL ATTRACTIONS: Revived ghost town of Madrid, Los Cerrillos, Golden, Santa Fe, Cibola National Forest, Sandia Mountain Wilderness, hiking.

LOCATION: North-central New Mexico. The drive begins at the junction of Interstate 40 and Highway 14 in Tijeras, just east of Albuquerque.

DRIVE ROUTE NUMBER: Highway 14.

TRAVEL SEASON: Year-round. Fall is probably the most pleasant time. Snows will occasion-ally cover the road in winter, especially on the south end of the route. Snow tires or chains may be necessary at those times; otherwise, the road is usually dry.

CAMPING: There are no public campgrounds along the drive. The Cibola National Forest operates several campgrounds in the Man-zano Mountains south of Tijeras.

SERVICES: All services are available in Santa Fe. Gas and food are available in Cedar Crest and Tijeras. Madrid has several restau-rants and limited lodging.

NEARBY ATTRACTIONS: Sandia Crest, Petro-glyph National Monument, Salinas Pueblo Missions National Monument.

THE DRIVE

The popular drive between Tijeras and Santa Fe has become known as the Turquoise Trail. Highway 14 is a much more attractive and less busy route between Santa Fe and Albuquerque than Interstate 25. It passes through several interesting towns and the foothills of three mountain ranges.

From I–40, the drive climbs north to Cedar Crest on the east side of the San-dia Mountains. Unlike the west side of the Sandias, an imposing wall of cliffs that towers over Albuquerque, the east side rises more gently and is heavily wooded with ponderosa pine on the lower slopes and fir, spruce, and aspen higher up. The massive faulting and earth movement that created the Rio Grande Valley lifted the Sandia Mountains almost 6,000 feet above the river. Most of the range lies in the **Cibola National Forest.** Hiking and skiing attract thousands of people to the mountains every year.

The town of Cedar Crest, just up the road from I–40, is largely a diffused sub-urb of Albuquerque. Many people commute into the city every day, evidenced by the four-lane width of Highway 14. The pines and mountain views have attracted many residents.

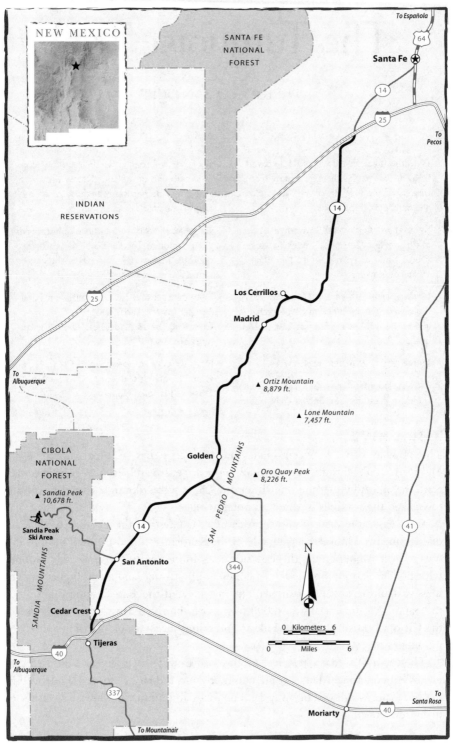

Adobe church in Golden

At the junction with Highway 536, the four-lane road and most of the traffic ends. Highway 536 climbs up to Sandia Crest on top of the Sandia Mountains. It's a beautiful side trip described in Drive 16.

After the junction with Highway 536, Highway 14 gradually descends away from the Sandia Mountains. The housing developments thin out, and the road enters quintessential New Mexico terrain—hills covered with stunted piñon-juniper forest under a vast indigo sky.

Golden, a tiny village in the San Pedro Mountains, had its start in 1879 as a gold-mining town. It lies at the south end of the oldest mining district in New Mexico. Gold was discovered in 1839 in the area, usually as loose particles and nuggets mixed with gravel in dry creek bottoms. Later, a new gold strike, plus discovery of lead and silver ores, created a short-lived boom and the founding of Golden. The mines never produced vast quantities of wealth, and a shortage of water made early mining attempts difficult; the town soon dwindled.

Today, a few homes and a gift shop or two make up the town. Junipers and cacti sprout from the collapsed stone walls of abandoned houses and businesses. The jewel of the village is the small adobe church perched on a hill by the highway. The old structure has recently been restored by local residents and painted a bright white. The church and graveyard have suffered some vandalism in the past, so local residents are touchy about visitors. Please be respectful if you visit the church.

Shops in the former ghost town of Madrid

MADRID AND LOS CERRILLOS

About 11 miles north of Golden, the town of **Madrid** is tucked into a small valley on the north side of the Ortiz Mountains. Madrid boomed on the basis of a much less glamorous, but more necessary, commodity—coal. Miners dug coal from the hills around Madrid as early as 1835 to fuel smelters at area gold mines. The arrival of railroads in New Mexico in the 1880s spurred demand for the high-quality hard coal found here. A short branch line of the Santa Fe Railroad was built into the town and the mines prospered. At one time, the town produced 250,000 tons of coal per year and was larger than Albuquerque.

Rows of wooden frame houses were built in the company town, many of which have been restored. The town boasted a golf course and tennis courts. It was so famed for its Christmas lights in the 1930s that TWA flights made detours to fly over the town. However, by 1947 coal demand had declined and the mines closed. The spur track was pulled up and the town slowly decayed. In 1975 the town's owner sold the weathered residences cheaply to artists and people searching for an alternative lifestyle. Madrid has experienced a steady renaissance and now has an array of shops, galleries, and restaurants. An old steam engine is parked in front of the Old Coal Mine Museum. The museum includes a coal mine and exhibits on the town's mining history.

A few miles north of Madrid, adobe homes and arching cottonwoods line the dusty streets of the village of **Los Cerrillos.** The sleepy atmosphere belies the town's bustling past. The surrounding hills disguise the oldest mining district in New Mexico and possibly the United States. Before the Spaniards arrived, Indians dug turquoise from a nondescript hill, Mount Chalchihuitl. Even with their primitive tools, they dug a pit 130 feet deep and 200 feet across at the top. Much of the turquoise in the hands of the Aztecs when Cortez conquered them in 1519 is believed to have come from Cerrillos and the Burro Mountains in southwestern New Mexico. Eventually, some of this turquoise even worked its way into the crown jewels of Spain.

The Spaniards continued small-scale turquoise mining, plus lead and possibly silver mining. The first gold rush in the American West started in 1828 when gold was discovered in the nearby Ortiz Mountains. A second gold strike was made in the San Pedro Mountains in 1839. Modest activity continued throughout much of the nineteenth century until new silver, lead, and gold finds brought a new boom to the area for a few years in the 1880s. Today, only small-scale mining occurs for the most part. The picturesque old buildings and dirt streets help Los Cerrillos mine for gold in Hollywood now. A number of movies have been filmed here, including *Young Guns.*

After Los Cerrillos, the highway climbs north through sandstone hills and then grasslands to Santa Fe. The drive ends at the south side of town, at the junction with I–25.

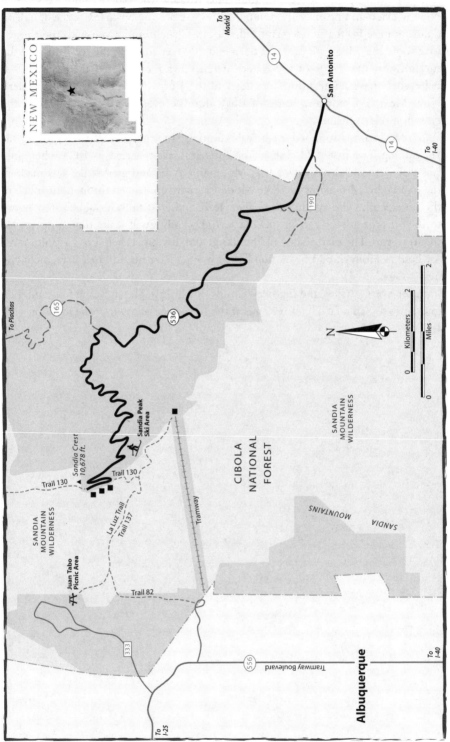

Sandia Crest Scenic Byway

SAN ANTONITO TO SANDIA CREST

GENERAL DESCRIPTION: A 14-mile drive from scrubby piñon-juniper forest to tremendous views and lush subalpine forest on the highest highway in New Mexico.

SPECIAL ATTRACTIONS: Sandia Crest, Sandia Peak Tramway, Sandia Mountain Wilderness, Sandia Peak Ski Area, Cibola National Forest, Sandia Man, Tinkertown, hiking, fall color, views.

LOCATION: North-central New Mexico. The drive starts at the junction of Highway 536 and Highway 14 in San Antonito, a small town a few miles east of Albuquerque.

DRIVE ROUTE NUMBER: Highway 536.

TRAVEL SEASON: Year-round. The best time for the drive is summer and fall. Sandia Crest is usually cool and pleasant even at the height of summer. The mountains receive heavy snows in winter and temperatures can fall well below zero. The road is plowed but will sometimes be closed for a short time after a heavy snow. Depending on conditions, chains or snow tires may be required.

CAMPING: No car camping is allowed in the Sandia Mountains. Backpackers may use primitive camps in the wilderness. However, the Cibola National Forest does maintain several campgrounds in the Manzano Mountains south of Tijeras.

SERVICES: Food and gas are available in Cedar Crest and Tijeras. All services are available in nearby Albuquerque.

NEARBY ATTRACTIONS: Petroglyph National Monument, Salinas Pueblo Missions National Monument, Manzano Mountains, former ghost town of Madrid.

THE DRIVE

The paved highway to the top of the **Sandia Mountains** is one of the most spectacular drives in New Mexico. The road ends at the highest point in the Sandia Mountains, the 10,678-foot Sandia Crest. Although the Sandia Mountains are not large in area, they are high and even have a ski area. The mountains form a stunning backdrop to Albuquerque, their imposing cliffs towering more than a mile above the city. The views, combined with close proximity to Albuquerque, attract many thousands of people every year to Sandia Crest.

The mountains are a huge fault block that tilts upward to the west. The west side was severed by a fault from a huge block of crust that sank along the Rio Grande Valley. The valley marks a major break in the earth's crust known as the Rio Grande

Rift. A long sliver of crust that runs through central New Mexico dropped thousands of feet between two deep, irregular fault zones. The limestone that caps the top of the Sandia Mountains is also buried about 20,000 feet below the Rio Grande. Combined with the height of the mountains, the fault moved the two blocks of crust an incredible 26,000 feet, or 5 miles, apart.

The drive climbs up the east side of the mountains, a more gentle slope than the cliffs of the west side. From the junction of Highway 14 and Highway 536 in San Antonito, begin the steep, winding drive up Highway 536. The highway passes though several life zones as it climbs to the summit, replicating a drive from New Mexico to Canada. The road starts in piñon-juniper foothills and climbs through the transition zone, where ponderosa pine dominates, and the Canadian zone, where Douglas fir and aspen are common, to end at the Hudsonian zone dominated by Engelmann spruce and subalpine fir.

TINY TOWN

Tinkertown, a mile or so up the road from San Antonito, amuses people interested in miniature figures. Ross and Carla Ward have created an entire western town and circus in miniature. The walls surrounding the museum were built using more than 40,000 bottles. It is open daily from April 1 to November 1.

Shortly thereafter, the road passes a cluster of picnic areas. Several trailheads along the highway lead into the **Sandia Mountain Wilderness,** a scenic 37,232-acre area of the mountains to the north and south of the highway. Hikers use the trails in summer and cross-country skiers use them in winter.

As you climb, notice that the vegetation on the north-facing slopes is more lush. Because it receives less sun, it stays cooler and moister. New views to the east open up with every turn. The highway passes the base of the downhill ski area at about 8,700 feet. Aspens turn the mountain slopes gold in fall.

After 7.5 miles, you pass the junction with Highway 165. It is a winding gravel road that descends to the small town of Placitas and the Rio Grande Valley north of Albuquerque. Along the way, it passes **Sandia Man Cave,** an important archaeological site where traces of Sandia Man were discovered. A short trail leads to the small cave that sheltered prehistoric hunters 12,000 years ago. These early people roamed the Rio Grande Valley hunting many animals that are now extinct, such as the camel, woolly mammoth, and giant bison.

TO THE TOP

The highway passes two more picnic areas before reaching the crest. After parking the car, don't run to the overlook. The high altitude will have you puffing soon enough. Be sure to carry a jacket; it's often chilly even in summer. The drive up offers broad views to the east. From the top, a vertigo-inducing plunge down the western slope of the mountains opens up views in all directions. The city of Albuquerque and its suburbs sprawl from the base of the mountains to the other side of

Sandia Mountains, Cibola National Forest

the Rio Grande. Eighty miles west, Mount Taylor rises into the sky. To the north tower the Jemez and Sangre de Cristo Mountains.

Scenic hiking trails follow the crest for many miles north and south of the overlook. Hardy hikers can climb up to **Sandia Crest** from the city on the popular La Luz Trail. The strenuous trail climbs almost 4,000 feet in about 7.5 miles. Believe it or not, a footrace is held on the La Luz Trail every year. An easier hike involves a 1-mile walk south along the crest to the top terminal of the **Sandia Peak Tramway.** The trail passes fir and spruce trees twisted and bent from exposure to strong, frequent winds on the mountain top. Enjoy lunch at the High Finance Restaurant before walking back. The tramway, the longest in the United States, carries people 2.7 miles from the foothills to the top of the mountain.

Plan to stay at Sandia Crest until sunset. As the sun slowly sinks into the horizon, the valley falls into shadow and the Rio Grande becomes a silvery ribbon reflecting the western sky. The crest turns gold and then pink in the last rays of the sun. Dusk falls after the sun slips out of sight, and Albuquerque becomes a twinkling blanket of lights far below.

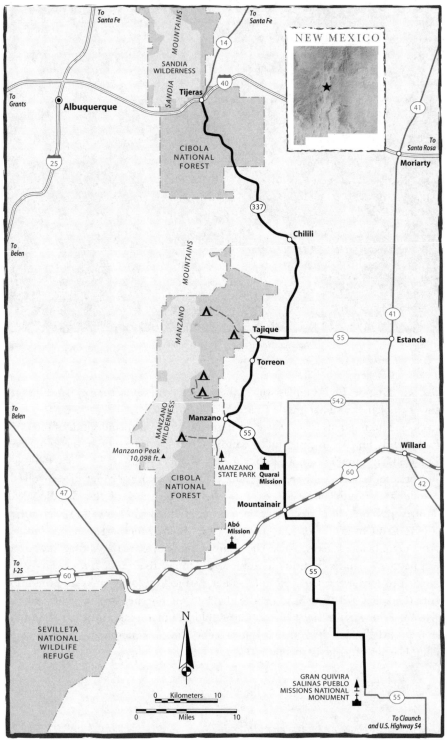

NEW MEXICO

To Santa Fe

To Santa Fe

14

SANDIA WILDERNESS

SANDIA MOUNTAINS

40

Tijeras

To Grants

● Albuquerque

CIBOLA NATIONAL FOREST

25

41

To Santa Rosa

Moriarty

337

To Belen

Chilili

MANZANO MOUNTAINS

Tajique

55

Estancia

41

Torreon

542

MANZANO WILDERNESS

Manzano

55

Willard

To Belen

Manzano Peak 10,098 ft. ▲

MANZANO STATE PARK

Quarai Mission

60

42

CIBOLA NATIONAL FOREST

47

Mountainair

Abó Mission

To 1-25

60

55

SEVILLETA NATIONAL WILDLIFE REFUGE

N

GRAN QUIVIRA SALINAS PUEBLO MISSIONS NATIONAL MONUMENT

55

0 Kilometers 10

0 Miles 10

To Claunch and U.S. Highway 54

Salinas Pueblo Missions National Monument

TIJERAS TO GRAN QUIVIRA

GENERAL DESCRIPTION: A 79-mile drive through Hispanic villages and old Spanish mission ruins in the foothills of the Manzano Mountains.

SPECIAL ATTRACTIONS: Salinas Pueblo Missions National Monument, Manzano Mountain Wilderness, Manzano Mountains, Cibola National Forest, Manzano State Park, fall color, hiking, camping.

LOCATION: North-central New Mexico. The drive starts at the junction of Highway 337 and Interstate 40 in Tijeras, a few miles east of Albuquerque.

DRIVE ROUTE NUMBER: Highway 337, Highway 55.

TRAVEL SEASON: Year-round. The drive is most pleasant in summer and fall. Winter snowstorms occasionally will make the drive slick and icy, necessitating the use of chains and snow tires, but usually the highway is dry. Thunderstorms are common in late summer.

CAMPING: The Cibola National Forest operates several campgrounds in the Manzano Mountains, including Fourth of July, New Canyon, Red Canyon, Tajique, and Capilla Peak, all of which are accessible from the east side of the mountains. There are also campsites at Manzano Mountains State Park. Primitive camping is allowed throughout most of the national forest.

SERVICES: All services can be found in Mountainair. Food and gas can be found in Tijeras and Cedar Crest. All services are available in nearby Albuquerque.

NEARBY ATTRACTIONS: Sandia Crest, Sandia Mountain Wilderness, Sandia Peak Ski Area, Petroglyph National Monument.

THE DRIVE

As this paved route winds its way through the foothills of the Manzano Mountains past old Spanish missions and small Hispanic villages, it takes you back in time. The drive starts in the I–40 traffic roaring down Tijeras Canyon just east of the modern city of Albuquerque and ends at the tranquil site of the abandoned Spanish mission and pueblo at Gran Quivira.

Immediately upon turning onto Highway 337 at the junction with I–40, the traffic diminishes and the noise and bustle of Albuquerque fade into the distance. The highway soon enters the Cibola National Forest as it winds up a canyon into the northern end of the **Manzano Mountains.** The vegetation is mostly piñon pine and juniper, but as the road climbs higher, ponderosa pine appears. Two picnic areas, Pine Flat and Oak Flat, are on the east side of the highway. After a few miles, the highway leaves the national forest and descends gradually toward the broad Estancia Valley.

The Estancia Valley is a grassy north-south–trending valley east of the Manzano Mountains. In Pleistocene times, with the increased precipitation of the ice age, the valley contained a large lake with no outlet. As the climate warmed and dried, the lake evaporated, leaving salt deposits, or *salinas*, in low points. This salt was important to Indians and Spanish settlers alike. Traces of the old lake's shoreline are still visible from the air.

The fertile soil of the lakebed once supported extensive farming, and towns such as Estancia and Willard thrived. Between 1900 and 1940, large amounts of pinto beans were cultivated in the valley. A railroad was built into the valley after the turn of the twentieth century to ship beans and other agricultural produce. It became known as the "Bean Line."

Unfortunately, steady erosion of the rich lakebed soil by plowing, combined with wind and rain, caused the eventual failure of most farms in the valley. Droughts in the 1930s and 1940s accelerated abandonment of the farmland. Towns like Willard now are only shadows of their former size.

CHILILI AND TAJIQUE

The little village of **Chilili** was founded near the site of an old Indian pueblo. In about 1618, Fray Alonso de Peinado established a small mission at the pueblo, but it was abandoned later that century. In 1839 Hispanic settlers living in the area received a land grant for the village of Chilili, but it was soon abandoned. The town arose again later in the nineteenth century near the old original pueblo. Today, Chilili remains a small village in an area known for land ownership disputes.

Ten miles south of Chilili, Highway 337 ends at a junction with Highway 55. Turn right toward **Tajique** and Mountainair. Like Chilili, Tajique was built at the site of an abandoned Tewa Indian pueblo. The ruins provided a source of ready-made building material for the Hispanic settlers. Tajique is the starting point for a worthwhile side trip in fall. Turn right, west, in the center of the village on Forest Road 55 and drive about 7 miles into the mountains to Fourth of July Campground, site of the largest stand of maples in New Mexico. In early to mid-October, the maples turn the hillsides many shades of deep scarlet, blazing orange, and golden yellow. Several trails lead into the 36,970-acre Manzano Mountain Wilderness. Although the Manzano Mountains appear small and uninteresting from a distance, in reality they are a heavily wooded range that rises more than 10,000 feet in elevation.

Just south of Tajique, Highway 55 passes through Torreon, yet another small Hispanic village built on the ruins of a Tewa pueblo. Apache raids, drought, famine, and disease forced the abandonment of many pueblos on the east side of the Manzano Mountains. "The Cities that Died of Fear" was one appellation given to these abandoned villages.

The next village along the highway is Manzano, settled in the early 1800s. *Manzano* means "apple" in Spanish. The town and the nearby mountains were named for apple trees found in the area when the town was founded. Apparently the trees had been planted some years earlier by unknown persons.

Forest Service roads lead east from Manzano to Red Canyon, New Canyon, and Capilla Peak campgrounds, along with several wilderness trailheads. Forest Road 253 also leads to **Manzano State Park.** The road to the fire lookout on 9,375-foot Capilla Peak is the only road to the crest of the mountains. A high-clearance vehicle may be necessary. Call the forest service for current conditions. The dirt road is steep, narrow, and winding and not recommended for trailers or other large recreation vehicles.

PUEBLO HISTORY

Just a few miles southeast of Manzano, the highway passes the first of three units of **Salinas Pueblo Missions National Monument.** Quarai, and the two other pueblos farther south at Abó and Gran Quivira, were the site of large multistory apartment-like masonry villages and Spanish missions. Although people had lived in the Estancia Valley for thousands of years, they did not start building aboveground stone pueblos until about the 1300s. The towns thrived with an economy based on farming, trade in salt and other items, and hunting. Coronado and other explorers first arrived in New Mexico in 1540. Although stories of the Spaniards no doubt circulated among these pueblos, they were not actually visited by them until after Oñate arrived in northern New Mexico in 1598. Their way of life was about to change forever.

The first Franciscan priest to move to the Estancia Valley settled in Chilili in 1618 to attempt conversion of that pueblo to Christianity. Four years later, Fray Francisco Fonte moved to Abó to establish a mission. Using plentiful red sandstone and timbers from the nearby mountains, Fonte enlisted the Indians in constructing the *convento* with its dining areas, storerooms, bedrooms, offices, workshops, and kitchens. He then oversaw the building of the church, a far larger structure than the Indians had ever seen.

In 1626 Fray Juan Gutierrez de la Chica arrived at the Quarai pueblo and began construction of the *convento* and church. He was ambitious and spent five years building one of the most impressive churches in New Mexico. The 5-foot-thick, 40-foot-high walls enclosed a cross-shaped space 100 feet long and 27 feet wide, with a transept 50 feet wide.

In 1629 Fray Francisco Letrado arrived at **Gran Quivira,** or *Las Humanas* as it was known then. He set up temporary quarters and a chapel in several abandoned rooms in the pueblo. He had just begun construction of the walls of the church and *convento* when he was transferred to Zuni in 1631. Fray Francisco Acevedo of the Abó mission oversaw completion of the small Gran Quivira church. Because of water shortages, Gran Quivira was not able to support a full-size mission; instead, it became a circuit church served by Abó.

Quarai church ruins, Salinas Pueblo Missions National Monument

In 1659 a new priest, Fray Diego de Santander, arrived at Gran Quivira to try to develop a full mission. However, Santander faced a losing battle. Conflicts between church and state officials escalated. Hostilities increased between the Spaniards and Apaches, leading to frequent raids of the pueblos. To compound the problems, severe drought struck the area in the 1660s and 1670s. Widespread famine and disease decimated the pueblos of the Estancia Valley. Although Santander and his successor finished the *convento* at Gran Quivira, the new, larger church was never completed.

In 1671 both Spaniards and Indians abandoned Gran Quivira. By 1673 stores of food ran out at Abó, and either Apaches or the Pueblo Indians burned the *convento*. The Spaniards fled, followed soon thereafter by the Indians. In 1677 even Quarai was abandoned, its surviving residents moving to the Rio Grande Valley and other parts of New Mexico. The Estancia Valley lay quiet for many years. The Pueblo Indians never returned, and Hispanic settlers did not come back until the nineteenth century.

Today, the hulking ruins of the church at Quarai are shaded by cottonwoods that rustle with the slightest breeze, and the extensive Indian pueblos have collapsed into mounds of rubble. A small visitor center describes the mission's history.

MOUNTAINAIR

South of Quarai, Highway 55 crosses U.S. Highway 60 in **Mountainair.** The small town was founded in 1901 when the Santa Fe Railroad built tracks through nearby Abó Pass. The main visitor center for Salinas Pueblo Missions National Monument is in Mountainair. While in Mountainair, be sure to visit the ruins of the Abó pueblo a few miles west of town on US 60. The ruins of the old church and *convento* have been excavated and stabilized. The red sandstone walls still rise almost 40 feet, and the springs that fostered the first settlement there still flow.

South of Mountainair, Highway 55 passes through low hills wooded with piñon and juniper. After about 25 miles, the highway passes Gran Quivira. The ruins huddle on a dry hilltop, partly masked by trees and shrubs. Some of the ruins have been excavated; others lie under piles of rubble dotted with cholla cacti. From the old church, look out across the empty country. Only a few ranches and park service buildings are visible in the broad sweep of terrain. The old Salinas Province of Spanish New Mexico was probably more heavily settled 360 years ago than it is now.

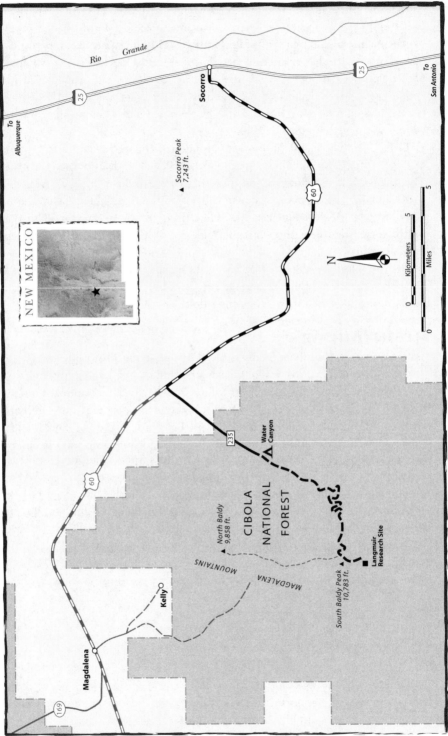

Magdalena Mountains

SOCORRO TO SOUTH BALDY

GENERAL DESCRIPTION: A 29-mile paved and gravel drive from Socorro in the Rio Grande Valley to the top of the rugged, forested Magdalena Mountains.

SPECIAL ATTRACTIONS: Cibola National Forest, Magdalena Mountains, Langmuir Research Site, Owl Bar, hiking, camping, fall color.

LOCATION: Central New Mexico. The drive starts on the south side of Socorro at the junction of U.S. Highway 60 and the main north-south business street through town, the Interstate 25 business route.

DRIVE ROUTE NUMBER: US 60, Forest Road 235.

TRAVEL SEASON: Summer and fall. Snows blanket the higher parts of the mountains in winter, closing the upper part of the road.

CAMPING: The Cibola National Forest manages the Water Canyon Campground along the route. Primitive camping is allowed throughout most of the national forest.

SERVICES: All services are available in Socorro.

NEARBY ATTRACTIONS: Ghost town of Kelly, Bosque del Apache National Wildlife Refuge, San Mateo Mountains, Very Large Array radio telescope.

THE DRIVE

The drive climbs 6,000 feet from the desert town of Socorro and the Rio Grande to the cool, forested peaks of the Magdalena Mountains. Along the way, it passes through several different life zones of vegetation and climate.

Unlike most drives in this book, which are paved, the last 8 miles of this route is on an improved dirt surface. The unpaved section is steep, narrow, and winding, so it's not recommended for trailers or large recreation vehicles. But because of the research labs on the summit, the road receives regular maintenance. Except after heavy rains, the road doesn't present any serious problems to most other vehicles, provided care is used. You may want to call the Forest Service for current conditions. The road is paved and easily traveled as far as the Water Canyon Campground.

SOCORRO'S HISTORY

The drive begins in **Socorro,** a Rio Grande Valley town of about 9,000 people. Don Juan de Oñate stopped at the Piro Indian pueblo at the current site of Socorro in 1598 on his journey north. The rest of his colonizing expedition was struggling through the desert behind him. The Piro Indians aided Oñate with food and water, leading to the pueblo's name *Socorro,* which means "aid" or "succor."

When Oñate continued north, two priests remained behind to do missionary work among the Indians. A church was built and the first grapes were planted in New Mexico. After the Pueblo Revolt of 1680, the village was abandoned. Spain reestablished rule in 1692, but Socorro remained deserted except for passing travelers on the Camino Real.

In 1816 Spain granted land around Socorro to twenty-one families. Farming and ranching supported these new residents, and Socorro also served as a way station along the Camino Real, or Chihuahua Road, as it later came to be called. Depending on the travelers' direction of travel, Socorro was the last stop before entering the Jornada del Muerto or first stop after crossing it. The Jornada del Muerto was a much-feared section of the Camino Real. To shorten the route between El Paso and Santa Fe, travelers cut across a 90-mile section of bare, almost waterless desert well away from the Rio Grande. Because many people died from thirst, heat, or Apache raids on the route, it became known as the *Jornada del Muerto,* or "Journey of Death."

In 1854, after New Mexico was ceded to the United States, Fort Craig was built along the river south of Socorro to defend against Indian raids. Socorro then prospered as a supply community. In 1862, during the Civil War, a contingent of Confederate troops from Texas defeated Union soldiers from the fort and marched north to Santa Fe to claim New Mexico for the Confederacy. Interestingly, and sadly, the Union leader, Edward Canby, and the Confederate leader, Henry Sibley, were friends and former West Point schoolmates. Canby even served as Sibley's best man when Sibley married.

Prospectors discovered lead-silver ores in the Magdalena Mountains west of Socorro in the 1860s, and mining started by 1870. The ores were smelted locally and shipped over the Santa Fe Trail to Kansas City. Development was slow until the railroad reached Socorro in 1881 and Magdalena and Kelly in 1883. With better transportation, the three towns grew rapidly. Because there were nearby supplies of coal and limestone, crucial for processing the lead-silver ore, smelters were built in Socorro to treat the output from the Kelly mines. Socorro became the territory's largest town by the early 1890s. The booming mining industry led the New Mexico legislature to establish the New Mexico School of Mines at Socorro in 1889. Unfortunately, by the time the school opened its doors, mine output was already declining. In 1893 silver prices collapsed, and the last smelter and many mines closed.

Socorro recovered from the mining bust and other reverses and thrives again today. The college, now known as the New Mexico Institute of Mining and Technology, offers degrees in mining engineering and many other technical professions. Socorro's Mineral Museum boasts thousands of gem, mineral, and fossil specimens.

Most visitors to Socorro see only the busy commercial strip in town. However, a small historic district centered around the town plaza exhibits many different styles of New Mexico architecture, from Indian pueblo adobe to territorial adobe

Breaking clouds over Cibola National Forest, Magdalena Mountains

to Victorian. The San Miguel church is located 3 blocks north of the plaza on the site of the original mission destroyed during the Pueblo Revolt.

SIDE TRIP FOR MUNCHIES

Before you start the drive west of Socorro, consider a side trip to the Owl Bar in San Antonio 10 miles south. The bar and restaurant is famous for its green chile hamburgers and cheeseburgers. San Antonio's other claim to fame is that it is the birthplace of hotelier Conrad Hilton. In his youth, Hilton helped his mother manage a hotel in San Antonio. After satisfying your appetite at the Owl Bar, go back to Socorro and head west on US 60.

The road climbs out of the river valley and around Socorro Peak along the abandoned grade of the railroad spur that ended at Magdalena and Kelly. The grasslands at the base of the looming Magdalena Mountains can be surprisingly lush and green in late summer.

About 15.5 miles west of Socorro, turn left on paved Forest Road 235 toward the mountains and Water Canyon Campground. The road leaves the grasslands and enters the mountains fairly abruptly. The lower slopes are wooded with piñon pine

Magdalena Mountains

and juniper, like most New Mexico mountains. The pavement ends at Water Canyon Campground, a pleasant spot to spend the night.

From the campground, the road continues up Water Canyon for about 2 miles and then begins to switchback up the mountain. Several signs along the road mark backcountry hiking trails. The road climbs through ponderosa pine and Douglas fir forest to the crest of the mountains. Views stretch in many directions. The last 2 or 3 miles pass through green meadows and patches of thick conifers. Here and there, aspens brighten the slopes on crisp autumn days. The drive ends at a gate a few hundred feet below 10,783-foot **South Baldy,** the highest point in the Magdalena Mountains. Beyond the gate, the road ends at **Langmuir Research Site,** a laboratory operated by the New Mexico Institute of Mining and Technology. Scientists there study lightning storms and other atmospheric phenomena. The small, but high, mountain range attracts thunderstorms that produce a lot of lightning, something to keep in mind if you are on the mountain top during a storm. A consortium including the Defense Department, New Mexico Institute of Mining and Technology, and other universities and labs has begun construction on the Magdalena Ridge Observatory near Langmuir. The facility will be a major site for astronomical research.

Be sure to try one of the hiking trails along the road before you drive back down the mountain. A favorite is Trail 8. It starts about half a mile before the gate and follows the crest of the mountains to North Baldy. The hike provides tremendous views almost the entire way. Remember, don't hurry; the air is thin at 10,000 feet.

Plains of San Agustin & the Beefsteak Trail

MAGDALENA TO APACHE CREEK

GENERAL DESCRIPTION: A 90-mile paved highway that traverses the Plains of San Agustin before crossing the Continental Divide.

SPECIAL ATTRACTIONS: Very Large Array Telescope, historic cattle trail, Cibola, Apache, and Gila National Forests, scenic views, camping.

LOCATION: Southwestern New Mexico. The drive starts in Magdalena, a small town about 27 miles west of Socorro.

DRIVE ROUTE NUMBER: U.S. Highway 60, Highway 12.

TRAVEL SEASON: Year-round. The route can be hot in summer and can receive heavy snows in winter. Late summer and early fall are ideal times.

CAMPING: The pleasant Datil Well Campground near Datil is the only developed campground along the route. It has water. Primitive camping is allowed throughout most of the national forests along the route.

SERVICES: All services are available at Magdalena and Datil (and Reserve, just beyond the end of the route). Gas is available in Aragon. These are very small towns in remote country. Do not count on obtaining gas or food late at night or on Sunday.

NEARBY ATTRACTIONS: Rock climbing at Enchanted Tower, Gila, Withington, and Apache Kid Wildernesses, ghost town of Kelly.

THE DRIVE

The highway from Magdalena to Apache Creek crosses some of the emptiest country in New Mexico. Most of the drive cuts through the middle of Catron County, the largest in the state but the least populated, with less than 3,000 people in 7,000 square miles. Much of the route crosses the lonely Plains of San Agustin. The grassy plains form a vast valley ringed by mountains on all sides.

The drive starts in **Magdalena,** an old mining, lumbering, and cattle-shipping center. Before you head west on US 60, consider taking a short side trip to the old ghost town of **Kelly.** From the Cibola National Forest office on US 60 in the center of town, drive south on the paved cross street that leads past the side of the offices. Go about 2 miles to a fork at the end of the pavement beyond the edge of

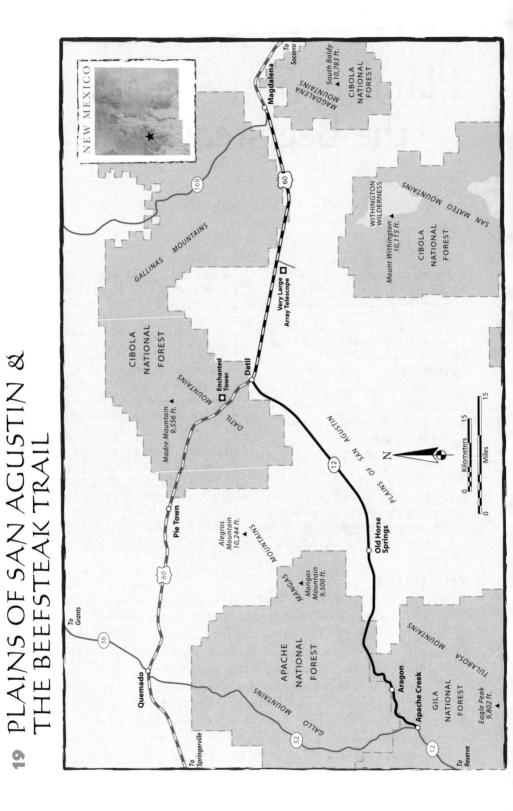

19 PLAINS OF SAN AGUSTIN & THE BEEFSTEAK TRAIL

town. To the right sprawl the ruins and tailings of a mining mill. Follow the well-maintained gravel left fork (Forest Road 304) 1.4 miles to the old church in Kelly.

Kelly was founded after the discovery of lead-silver ores in the 1860s on the slopes of the Magdalena Mountains. The town developed slowly until the railroad arrived in Socorro in 1881 and Magdalena in 1883. The mines boomed, producing most of the lead in New Mexico for twenty years. A large smelter was built in Socorro to handle the output from the Kelly mines and other area mines. Socorro grew quickly into a town of 5,000 people by the mid-1880s; Magdalena grew to 1,300 and Kelly to 800 people. Good supplies of coal and limestone near Socorro helped with smelting the ore. Another smelter was built between Kelly and Magdalena. Beginning in the 1890s, the boom began to subside, and most mining ending by 1931.

Aside from the white stucco church, little remains today of Kelly, other than foundations and a few stone walls. Old mines and rusting steel head frames dot the mountain slopes above the town site. Most of the mines are on private property; please respect the owners' wishes in regard to trespassing. Old mines are dangerous, so be very careful around open shafts and tunnels.

BEEFSTEAK TRAIL

Mining was not the only reason for the growth of Magdalena, however. The arrival of the railroad set up the town as the primary livestock shipping point for much of southwestern New Mexico. US 60 west of town follows the route of the old **Magdalena Stock Driveway,** or the "Beefsteak Trail." The highway slowly climbs west from Magdalena through a thin forest of piñon pine and juniper. A historic marker on the right, about 10 miles west of town, describes the stock driveway.

The first cattle drives along the 125-mile route began in 1885. The driveway forked in Datil, with one arm going to Horse Springs and the other extending all the way to Springerville, Arizona. The driveway was as much as 5 to 10 miles wide. The peak year was 1919, when 150,000 sheep and 21,677 cattle traveled the route. In the 1930s the Civilian Conservation Corps fenced the driveway and drilled water wells. When the highway arrived, trucking became more common as a method of moving livestock to market. But some cattlemen still preferred to drive the cattle to market because the stock arrived in better condition from grazing along the trail. Amazingly, the last portion of the driveway did not close until as recently as 1971, making it the last regularly used cattle trail in the United States.

About 12 miles west of Magdalena, the highway passes a marked turnoff on the left that leads to Mount Withington and the rugged San Mateo Mountains. The mountains, easily visible to the south of the highway, rise to more than 10,000 feet. The gravel road to the mountains is usually in good condition except after heavy rain or snow. Quiet campgrounds and the Withington and Apache Kid Wildernesses lie in the little-visited San Mateo Mountains.

After passing the Mount Withington turnoff, the road drops down slightly into the vast Plains of San Agustin. Although the plains are not spectacular in themselves, they give an incredible sense of the "wide-open spaces." In late summer thunderstorms tower into the sky, and rainbows arch down over the plains. Other than the radio telescope and a few widely scattered ranches and windmills, the sprawling plains are almost devoid of signs of mankind.

The plains are a large, flat, mountain-ringed valley created when a block of the earth's crust sank between parallel faults. Although the plains are lower than the surrounding mountains, they still lie at an average elevation of 7,000 feet. The climate is relatively pleasant even in the height of summer and can be very cold in winter.

TELESCOPE STOP

Before arriving in Datil, the highway crosses one spur of the railroad tracks that are used to move the twenty-seven antennas that make up the **Very Large Array (VLA) radio telescope.** Each antenna weighs 230 tons and has an 82-foot reflecting dish. The antennas are placed in varying configurations along a large Y-shaped set of railroad tracks. The VLA is the largest and most powerful radio telescope in the world. It has been used to study galaxies and quasars as far as ten billion light years away. The visitor center is open daily from 8:30 A.M. to sunset.

The tiny village of Datil lies at the fork of the old stock driveway. The pleasant Datil Well campground is just west of town and can be reached from either US 60 or Highway 12. At the highway intersection in the middle of town, you'll find a combined gas station, general store, bar, and cafe. Even the small motel is run out of this complex. The bar and cafe are true western rustic—pine plank walls with branding irons, animal trophies, saddles, and the like hung here and there. Unlike in some Albuquerque steak houses or urban cowboy bars, here it seems appropriate.

Rock climbers may want to take a side trip from Datil to explore one of the prime climbing spots in New Mexico, **Enchanted Tower.** Although the area is little-known outside of the state, it is becoming one of the classic hangouts for Albuquerque climbers. Go west of Datil on US 60 as it ascends through the Datil Mountains to the Continental Divide. At about 5 miles, turn right onto a good dirt road, Forest Road 59, marked by a sign, CLEAVELAND-GATLIN. The road goes 0.9 miles to a ranch. Turn left just before the ranch buildings onto a lesser, but still passable, road that turns up Thompson Canyon. After another 1.7 miles, you'll see the rocks on the right canyon wall. Enchanted Tower itself is a massive overhanging fin of rock that pokes out into the canyon. Some climbing routes with difficulty ratings as high as 5.13 have been established on the tower. Other adjoining cliffs have many other climbing routes.

Back on the main drive, go west on Highway 12 from Datil. The route follows the northwest side of the plains, occasionally ascending into mountain foothills. Finally, the highway climbs gradually out of the plains, into the Gila National Forest, and over the Continental Divide. Piñon and ponderosa pines and junipers blan-

The most powerful radio telescope in the world

ket the slopes. After crossing the divide, the highway slowly descends down the Tularosa River. The river cuts a route through a narrow canyon before opening up into a lush, narrow valley near the village of Aragon. The tiny town is the site of Fort Tularosa and a failed attempt to establish a reservation for a group of Apaches led by Cochise.

Past Aragon, the highway continues down the valley 7 more miles to the junction with Highway 32 at Apache Creek. Beyond Apache Creek, the drive can be continued by following the Glenwood to Quemado scenic drive in this guide.

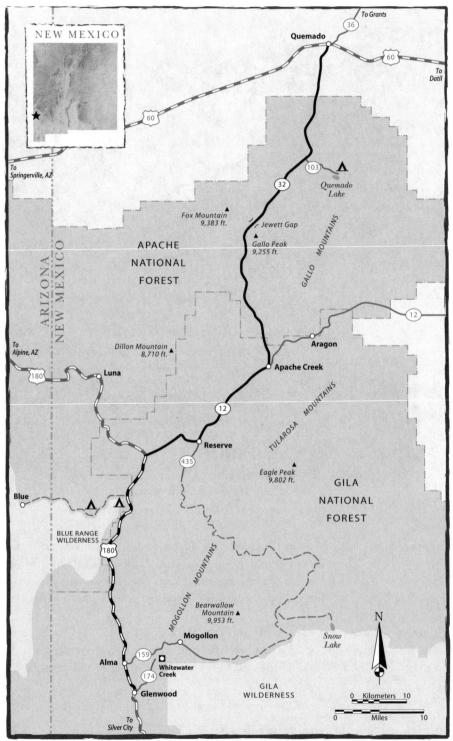

NEW MEXICO

To Grants

Quemado
36

60
To Datil

60

To Springerville, AZ

103

Quemado Lake

32

Fox Mountain
9,383 ft.

Jewett Gap

Gallo Peak
9,255 ft.

GALLO MOUNTAINS

APACHE

NATIONAL

FOREST

12

Dillon Mountain
8,710 ft.

Aragon

To Alpine, AZ

180
Luna

Apache Creek

12

TULAROSA MOUNTAINS

Reserve

435

Eagle Peak
9,802 ft.

GILA

NATIONAL

FOREST

Blue

BLUE RANGE
WILDERNESS

180

MOGOLLON MOUNTAINS

Bearwallow
Mountain
9,953 ft.

Mogollon

Snow
Lake

N

Alma

159

Whitewater
Creek

174

Glenwood

To Silver City

GILA
WILDERNESS

Kilometers   10

Miles   10

Southwestern Mountain Country

GLENWOOD TO QUEMADO

GENERAL DESCRIPTION: A 90-mile paved highway through the isolated mountain country of southwestern New Mexico.

SPECIAL ATTRACTIONS: Gila National Forest, Apache National Forest, Whitewater Creek, the Catwalk, Quemado Lake, hiking, fishing, camping, fall color.

LOCATION: Southwest New Mexico. The drive begins in Glenwood, about 60 miles northwest of Silver City on U.S. Highway 180.

DRIVE ROUTE NUMBER: US 180, Highway 12, Highway 32.

TRAVEL SEASON: Year-round. The most pleasant times are late summer, when thunderstorms turn the area a lush green, and fall when the cottonwoods change color. Winter can be cold, especially on the northern part of the drive. Snow can sometimes make driving treacherous after storms.

CAMPING: The Forest Service maintains several campgrounds along the drive, including Bighorn, Cottonwood, and Pueblo Park. Primitive camping is allowed throughout most of the rest of the forest.

SERVICES: All services are available, although limited, in Glenwood, Reserve, and Quemado.

NEARBY ATTRACTIONS: Ghost town of Mogollon, Snow Lake, Willow Creek, Gila Wilderness.

THE DRIVE

This drive passes through mountainous, lightly populated Catron County. Forests of ponderosa and piñon pine and juniper blanket most of the area along the route. The drive passes through part of the 3.3 million–acre Gila National Forest and a section of the Apache National Forest administered by the Gila National Forest. Ancient volcanoes created a vast, interconnected series of mountain ranges in this part of New Mexico and adjoining Arizona. Scattered hot springs are reminders that hot magma lies just under the surface.

The rugged land did not encourage settlement. The drive passes through three of the largest towns in Catron County, Glenwood, Reserve, and Quemado; but none is larger than 200 or 300 people. The old mining town of Mogollon once had a much bigger population, but it has dwindled to a ghost of its former self. Logging, ranching, and tourism are the primary engines driving the local economy today.

The drive starts in **Glenwood,** an attractive community located in a deep valley carved by the San Francisco River. The Mogollon Mountains just to the east rise to almost 11,000 feet. Most of the mountains lie within the 558,000-acre Gila Wilderness, the largest wilderness in the Southwest. Dense forests of spruce, fir, and aspen cover the upper slopes.

An interesting introduction to the Mogollon Mountains and the Gila Wilderness is just east of Glenwood. Before you start on the scenic drive, take a little side trip first. Look for signs in Glenwood to Whitewater Creek, the Catwalk, and Highway 174. Follow paved Highway 174 about 5 miles to its end at the Whitewater Picnic Ground.

WHITEWATER CREEK HIKE

The sparkling waters of **Whitewater Creek** rush down through a grove of enormous sycamores that shade the picnic area. A highly developed, unique Catwalk trail follows the creek upstream into a rocky gorge. Because the gorge is so narrow, the stream occupies the entire canyon bottom. To keep the trail out of the creek, it has been suspended on a catwalk, or a series of steel bridges, that cling to the canyon walls. After the initial catwalk, the trail crosses several other bridges, one quite sizable. The trail climbs up and down the rugged canyon walls, passing waterfalls and deep pools. It ends after crossing a small suspension bridge that sways as you cross it; kids love it. A new trail was recently built that is wheelchair-accessible.

Along the hike, look for large pieces of iron pipe in the canyon bottom and rusted bolts and concrete foundations on the cliffs. Before the turn of the century, the small town of Graham was located at the picnic ground. It was founded to process ore taken from mines in the mountains above Whitewater Creek. A water pipeline was built down the creek in 1893 to supply the town and mill. Like the trail, it was suspended from the canyon walls. A narrow walkway on top of the pipe formed a catwalk for repairmen. Floods have washed away all but the mill foundations in Graham.

The **Catwalk trail** is quite popular in summer. To leave the crowds behind, continue up the creek on Trail 207. It turns off the Catwalk trail just before the suspension bridge. The trail leads up into the heart of the Gila Wilderness by following the two main forks of Whitewater Creek.

After you return from your hike at Whitewater Creek, stop in for some down-home cooking at the Blue Front Bar and Cafe. Start the drive by heading north on US 180. The Forest Service maintains Bighorn Campground on the north side of Glenwood by the highway. It's convenient, but can be hot and noisy.

The highway climbs partway out of the San Francisco River valley to the junction of Highway 159. If you have time, consider taking a side trip on Highway 159

The Catwalk suspension bridge above Whitewater Creek

to the former ghost town of Mogollon, Snow Lake, Willow Creek, and the lush Mogollon Mountains. See Drive 21 for details.

IT'S ALL IN THE NAME

After the junction, US 180 drops back down to the San Francisco River valley at the small village of Alma. In fall the cottonwoods that line the river can turn brilliant gold. After several miles the highway crosses the river and climbs up onto Gut Ache Mesa. Early settlers seemed to favor this sort of place name in the Gila area. Take a close look at the Gila National Forest map or a topographic map. Other interesting names include Buzzard Canyon, Dead Man Spring, Bonanza Bill Flat, Jerky Mountains, Carcass Basin, Hogwallow Spring, High Lonesome Canyon, Rawmeat Creek, and Blow Fly Spring. The devil must not have been far away in those difficult early days. Devils Den Canyon, Hells Hole, Devils Spring, Diablo Range, and Devils Creek are but a few devil-related place names.

The highway steadily climbs north, reaching a high point at Saliz Pass. Ponderosa pines, with their dull orange, vanilla-scented bark and long needles, become more common with the increased altitude. After the pass, the road drops down into a deep canyon that usually has a running stream. The small Cottonwood Campground is on the west side of the highway. A mile or so past the campground, Forest Road 232 turns left, or west. To get to Pueblo Park Campground, follow the good gravel road about 6 miles. Tall ponderosa pines shade the small, quiet campground.

A few miles past the Pueblo Park turnoff is the junction with Highway 12. Turn right on Highway 12 and drop back down to the San Francisco River valley and the county seat of Reserve. Several routes lead deep into the **Gila National Forest** from Reserve. Highway 435 follows the river valley south from town before climbing up into the Tularosa and Mogollon Mountains. The well-maintained road leads to Willow Creek, Snow Lake, and many other destinations. The road can serve as a beautiful, but considerably longer, return route to Glenwood.

RESERVE TO QUEMADO

From Reserve, continue northeast on Highway 12 to the junction of Highway 32 at the tiny settlement of Apache Creek. Turn left on Highway 32 and drive north up the narrow valley cut by Apache Creek. The valley is pretty, with pastures, occasional ranches, and tall cottonwoods. After a number of miles, the highway climbs steeply out of the valley and then climbs slowly toward the Gallo Mountains through groves of ponderosa pines. Views open up of much of the surrounding country.

At Jewett Gap in the Gallo Mountains, the road reaches another high point. Pines shade a pleasant picnic area at the gap. After the gap, the road begins a long, slow descent from the Gallo Mountains. Along the way it passes a turnoff to **Quemado Lake,** Highway 103. The lake lies only a few miles off the highway and is worthy of a side trip. Camping and fishing are popular at the small lake tucked into a valley surrounded by sparsely wooded hills. An easy walk around the lake will stretch your legs before continuing the drive.

The highway continues its gradual descent to the small town of **Quemado.** The village was founded in a broad, open valley in about 1880. The area is notorious for being cold in winter, with temperatures sometimes falling far below zero. Quemado lies on the historic Magdalena Livestock Driveway, the last regularly used cattle trail in the United States. See Drive 19 for details. The town has limited food, gas, and lodging to serve your needs before you continue your trip.

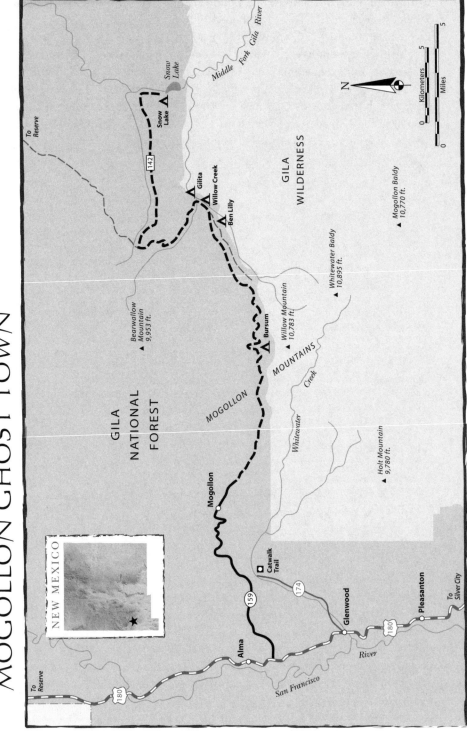

Gila Wilderness & Mogollon Ghost Town

ALMA TO SNOW LAKE

GENERAL DESCRIPTION: A 37-mile-long paved and gravel road that climbs into the lush high country of the Mogollon Mountains.

SPECIAL ATTRACTIONS: Snow Lake, ghost town of Mogollon, Gila Wilderness, Gila National Forest, hiking, camping, scenic views, fishing, fall color.

LOCATION: Southwestern New Mexico. The drive begins about 4 miles north of Glenwood at the intersection of U.S. Highway 180 and Highway 159. Glenwood is about 60 miles northwest of Silver City along US 180.

DRIVE ROUTE NUMBER: Highway 159, Forest Road 142.

TRAVEL SEASON: Late spring through fall. Heavy snowfall closes the road from the first storms in winter until spring. Otherwise, the road is usually dry except after summer thunderstorms.

CAMPING: Five Forest Service campgrounds lie along the route. Primitive camping is allowed elsewhere in the Gila National Forest.

SERVICES: All services are available in Glenwood. Food or snacks can sometimes be obtained in Mogollon but should not be relied upon.

NEARBY ATTRACTIONS: The Catwalk at Whitewater Creek, San Francisco Hot Springs.

THE DRIVE

This road winds through the highest mountains in southwestern New Mexico, ending at a small mountain lake. Except where it crosses a few small inholdings of private land, the entire route lies within the enormous 3.3-million-acre Gila National Forest. It climbs rapidly from grasslands dotted with piñon pine and juniper to mountain slopes blanketed with dense forests of Douglas fir and aspen.

The **Gila National Forest** encompasses a vast area of mountain highlands north of Silver City. Large Tertiary-age volcanoes ejected huge quantities of lava and ash, building a large area of interconnected mountain ranges, including the Black, Mogollon, Pinos Altos, Diablo, Tularosa, and other ranges. Of these, the Mogollon range is highest, reaching its peak at almost 11,000 feet at Whitewater Baldy. The area is very lightly inhabited. Believe it or not, the village of Glenwood is one of the biggest settlements in Catron County.

This drive is paved to Mogollon and then turns into a good all-weather gravel road that easily can be negotiated by most passenger cars. However, much of the road is very narrow and winding. In places there are blind corners when the road is not much more than one lane wide. I recommend lightly tapping your horn as you approach these curves to warn oncoming traffic, and to not take large recreation vehicles or trailers on this route.

From the intersection of US 180 and Highway 159, go west on Highway 159. The road quickly climbs up onto a broad, open mesa with views in all directions. After crossing the mesa, the road begins climbing in earnest, winding up the steep slopes of the Mogollon Mountains. Views quickly become spectacular. The Blue Range of New Mexico and Arizona lines the western horizon.

INTO MOGOLLON

After several blind curves, the road reaches a high point and drops down into **Mogollon.** The tiny town is squeezed into a steep, narrow canyon. In 1875 Sergeant James Cooney of the U.S. Cavalry discovered an outcrop of gold-bearing ore while rescuing a party of the U.S. Geological Survey that was being attacked by Apache Indians. After his military service ended, he returned to stake his claim. Some ore was shipped to Silver City by 1879, but fighting between the miners and Apaches slowed development. Cooney himself was killed in one battle. After the Apaches were defeated, the town boomed. Saloons, one named the Bloated Goat, and bordellos sprang up to serve the rip-roaring town. There was no jail in the wild early days of the mining camp, but plenty of criminals. Minor offenders were chained to a cottonwood tree. Those accused of more heinous crimes were hung from the same tree.

Gold poured from the mines during the 1890s, making the town the largest gold producer in New Mexico during that decade. Substantial silver, copper, and lead were also recovered. After the turn of the century, the rich ores dwindled and the town declined. Two revivals during the twentieth century helped keep some mining going until World War II. A few hardy residents remained in Mogollon, but the town nearly died. Most buildings deteriorated or were salvaged for building materials. In recent years, a few escapees from civilization have resettled Mogollon, rebuilding old structures and adding a few new ones. The high gold and silver prices of the late 1970s and early 1980s even spurred some sporadic mining efforts. Today, a few houses and tourist-oriented businesses line the narrow canyon bottom of Silver Creek. Old mine workings, ruined buildings, and foundations dot the hillsides above.

After Mogollon, the road becomes gravel-surfaced and climbs up Silver Creek, a small, relatively permanent stream. The forest becomes thick and lush, with ponderosa pine, Douglas fir, and aspen. After several switchbacks, the road reaches the 9,000-foot level just before Silver Creek Divide. After the divide, the road contours along the north slope of Willow Mountain for several miles. Along the way it passes

Buildings in the partly revived ghost town of Mogollon

a trailhead at Sandy Point, one of the most popular entry points of the **Gila Wilderness.**

If you have time and energy, be sure to hike at least partway up the trail. The trail follows the high crest of the Mogollon Range for 12 miles to Mogollon Baldy. It passes by flowing springs and old-growth forest with enormous Douglas firs, aspens, and Engelmann spruces. The Gila Wilderness covers 558,000 acres, making it the largest in the Southwest. At the urging of Aldo Leopold, the area was set aside in 1924 as the first designated wilderness in the United States. It protects much of the watershed of the Gila River.

CAMPGROUNDS TO TRY

Just beyond Sandy Point lies the small, two-site Bursum Campground. Along the road, gaps in the forest present broad views to the north across ranges of forested mountains. Several miles beyond Bursum Campground, the road descends to a much flatter mountain slope, where the road straightens out. After a total of about 27 miles from US 180, the road drops down to Willow Creek. A short side road leads to the Willow Creek and Ben Lilly campgrounds. These campgrounds do not have drinking water, so be sure to bring some or purify the creek water before use.

The crystal-clear creek tumbles down from the high crest of the Mogollon Mountains, carrying trout in its cold waters. Blue spruce and Douglas fir line the narrow valley.

About 3 miles beyond the Willow Creek turnoff, go right on FR 142, marked with signs for **Snow Lake.** This good road descends gradually through ponderosa pine forest to the valley of the Middle Fork of the Gila River. Idyllic Snow Lake lies in a broad, grassy valley encircled by ponderosa-covered hills. Small boats are allowed on the little lake, and a campground is tucked under the pines on a hill above.

The drive is long and winding, but worth the effort. The area is rarely crowded, except on holiday weekends in summer. Even a holiday weekend is less busy than a normal summer day in the mountains around Ruidoso, Santa Fe, or Taos.

The main road continues north into Reserve. Another route goes north and east to Beaverhead on what is called the Outer Loop. The Outer Loop is very scenic, but long and isolated. Take plenty of food, gas, and water. The road conditions can vary considerably depending on the weather and maintenance. Be sure to check with the Forest Service before attempting it. Sometimes it is not passable with a passenger car.

The Inner Loop Scenic Byway

SILVER CITY TO GILA CLIFF DWELLINGS

GENERAL DESCRIPTION: A 118-mile round-trip loop to ancient cliff dwellings, a former ghost town, and an enormous copper mine.

SPECIAL ATTRACTIONS: Gila Cliff Dwellings National Monument, Gila Wilderness, Gila National Forest, Santa Rita mine, former ghost town of Pinos Altos, hiking, camping, fishing, scenic views.

LOCATION: Southwestern New Mexico. The loop starts in Silver City.

DRIVE ROUTE NUMBER: Highway 15, Highway 35, Highway 152, and U.S. Highway 180.

TRAVEL SEASON: Year-round. The road is usually dry except during late summer thunderstorms and occasional winter snows. Snow tires or chains may occasionally be necessary during and after winter storms, but road problems are usually short-lived. Highway 15 is more prone to snow and ice problems than the rest of the loop.

CAMPING: Multiple Forest Service campgrounds are along the route a few miles past Pinos Altos, at the Gila River confluence near Gila Hot Springs, at Gila Cliff Dwellings National Monument, and at Lake Roberts. Primitive camping is allowed in the national forest along the route.

SERVICES: All services are available in Silver City. Food, limited lodging, and an RV campground can be found in Pinos Altos. A store and limited lodging are located at Gila Hot Springs. A store and limited lodging are located at Lake Roberts. Limited food and lodging can be found at the junction of Highway 15 and Highway 35. Food and gas can be found in the Mimbres Valley and in the Hanover/Central area.

NEARBY ATTRACTIONS: Black Range, Aldo Leopold Wilderness, City of Rocks State Park.

THE DRIVE

The paved loop begins in **Silver City,** one of the most important mining towns in the United States. Indians mined turquoise from the Burro Mountains southwest of Silver City long before the Spaniards set foot in New Mexico. Copper deposits at Santa Rita, east of Silver City, were discovered in 1798 by an Apache who relayed the information to Colonel Manuel Carrasco. Because he did not have the resources to develop the find himself, Col. Carrasco interested a wealthy Chihuahua merchant, Don Francisco Manuel Elguea, in investing. With Elguea's influence, the two men received the Santa Rita del Cobre Grant.

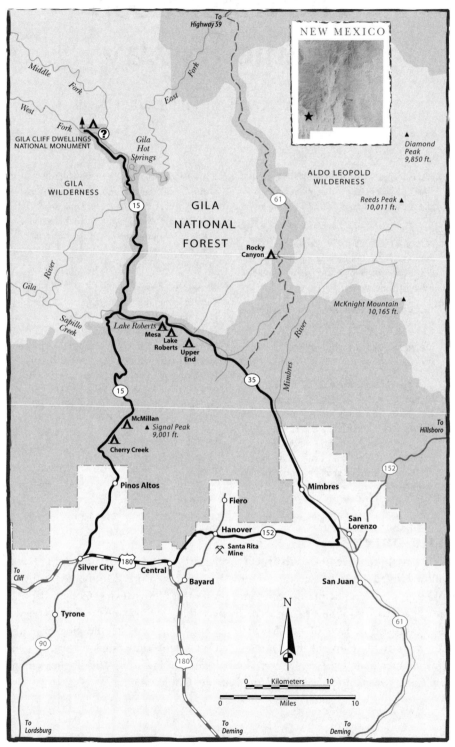

To Highway 59

Middle Fork

West Fork

East Fork

GILA CLIFF DWELLINGS NATIONAL MONUMENT

?

Gila Hot Springs

GILA WILDERNESS

15

Gila River

Sapillo Creek

NEW MEXICO

★

Diamond Peak 9,850 ft.

ALDO LEOPOLD WILDERNESS

Reeds Peak 10,011 ft.

GILA NATIONAL FOREST

61

Rocky Canyon

McKnight Mountain 10,165 ft.

Mimbres River

Lake Roberts
Mesa
Lake Roberts
Upper End

15

35

McMillan
Signal Peak 9,001 ft.

Cherry Creek

Pinos Altos

Fiero

Mimbres

To Hillsboro

152

San Lorenzo

Hanover

152

Santa Rita Mine

Silver City

180

Central

Bayard

San Juan

To Cliff

Tyrone

90

180

N

61

To Lordsburg

To Deming

To Deming

Kilometers 0 10

Miles 0 10

In 1804 Elguea bought out Carrasco and obtained a contract to supply copper to the Royal Mint in Mexico City. Elguea built crude smelters that could refine the high-quality ore before shipment to Mexico City, 1,300 miles away. For several years, the mine sent as many as 200 mule trains of copper annually to Mexico City. That amounted to an incredible six million pounds per year under very primitive frontier conditions. After Elguea died in 1809, mining came to a halt due to transportation problems, the Mexican Revolution, hostilities with local Indians, and declining demand. Only minor, sporadic copper mining occurred until after 1880.

In 1859 gold was discovered at **Pinos Altos.** The town boomed overnight, attracting gold seekers from far and wide. At Georgetown, a ghost town today, silver was discovered in 1866 and another town boomed. Rich silver ores were discovered just west of Silver City in 1870. In 1871 the old Indian turquoise mines in the Burro Mountains were rediscovered and mining began on a small scale. Silver City became the commercial center of the area's mining activity and remains so today. Two enormous open pit copper mines still operate at the site of the Indian turquoise mines in the Burro Mountains and at the Spanish mines at Santa Rita. Other smaller mines operate sporadically. The mining district is still one of the biggest copper producers in the United States.

Within Silver City there is a historical tour, and there are several museums. Many old brick and adobe buildings from the late 1800s have survived to the present day. Billy the Kid lived here for a while, and several sites mark his escapades.

The pleasant **Big Ditch Park** was created by floods around the turn of the twentieth century. Catastrophic flooding caused by heavy rains and overgrazing and over-harvesting of timber in the Pinos Altos Range dug a 55-foot-deep trench down what used to be the main street.

SAFETY FIRST

All of the drive is paved, but the section of Highway 15 between Pinos Altos and the junction with Highway 35 is very narrow, winding, and steep. There is no center line, the road is really only about one and one-half lanes wide, and there are several blind curves. Although it is one of the most scenic parts of the drive, it is not recommended for large recreation vehicles or trailers. Consider tapping your horn as you approach the blind corners to warn oncoming motorists. The section of Highway 15 after the junction with Highway 35 is also windy and steep but has a centerline and is a full two lanes wide. The rest of the loop is not particularly difficult. Although the distance from Silver City to the cliff dwellings is only 45 miles, allow about two hours for the drive.

Start the loop by driving north on Highway 15 to Pinos Altos. The road quickly climbs into the Pinos Altos Range. First juniper and piñon pine dot the slopes, then the taller ponderosa pines appear as you approach the little village. After the gold mining boom, the town almost sank into oblivion, but a few residents hung on. At an elevation of 7,000 feet, straddling the Continental Divide, the town is growing

Pinos Altos Opera House

slowly today as a cool mountain retreat. Several buildings remain from the town's boom days. The rustic Buckhorn Saloon is one of the classier restaurants in the Silver City area. For very homey, comfortable accommodations, possibly the best in the area, try the Bear Creek Cabins. Individual cabins are hidden here and there in a patch of tall ponderosa pines. Upstairs sleeping lofts and private porches and balconies add to the charm.

After Pinos Altos, the road narrows and winds deep into the Pinos Altos Range. Along the way, it passes an old Spanish *arrastra,* used to crush ore during the early mining days of Pinos Altos. A few miles beyond, a parking lot marks a short trail that leads to a memorial dedicated to Ben Lilly, a famous hunter in the early twentieth century in the Gila area. The road then climbs up Cherry Creek. Pines, cottonwoods, cherry trees, and some Douglas fir line the stream. Usually there is at least some flow in the creek. Two small campgrounds lie along the creek. The highway cuts through a gap in the Pinos Altos Range at the head of Cherry Creek and proceeds through pine forest along the north side of the Pinos Altos Range for several miles. It then drops precipitously downward to Sapillo Creek and the junction with Highway 35.

AROUND THE LOOP

Highway 35 will be the route used for the return. Highway 15, now a wider, easier road, immediately begins climbing up again toward the cliff dwellings. It winds up Copperas Creek, past pines and hillsides of dull orange and yellow soil. Be sure to stop at Copperas Vista, a pull-out at the high point of the highway. The canyon of the Gila River lies about 2,000 feet below. The **Gila Wilderness** sprawls out as far as the eye can see to the west. This dead-end highway leading to the cliff dwellings is surrounded by the 558,000-acre Gila Wilderness. On the western horizon looms the Mogollon Range, the tallest mountains in southwestern New Mexico with peaks almost 11,000 feet high. Other than the highway at Gila Hot Springs far below, there is not a sign of man to be seen.

After Copperas Vista, the highway descends steeply, meeting the Gila River at the confluence with the East Fork. A primitive campground with minimal facilities lies at the confluence. After a mile, the road passes by a store and a few homes in Gila Hot Springs. As occurs in several places in the Gila area, magma lies close enough to the surface here to heat underground water and form hot springs.

CLIFF DWELLINGS

The highway follows the Gila River upstream for about 3 miles to a fork. The right fork goes to the **Gila Cliff Dwellings National Monument** visitor center. You may want to stop there first. The left fork passes two small campgrounds with water before ending at the cliff dwellings.

Be sure to take the 1-mile loop trail to the dwellings. It climbs steeply 180 feet to large caverns eroded from the volcanic rock. A number of masonry ruins are tucked into these caves. Archaeologists believe that a late cultural stage of the

Gila Cliff Dwellings National Monument

Mogollon people built their homes here between about A.D. 1270 and 1290. After a few decades, these people abandoned their dwellings for unknown reasons. Researchers speculate that some combination of drought, warfare, depletion of natural resources, or internal social schism may have spurred the exodus.

The cliff dwellings area is one of the prime entry points of the Gila Wilderness with several trailheads. Two of the most popular are the West Fork trail that begins at the cliff dwellings parking lot and the Middle Fork trail that starts near the visitor center. All of the trails lead to clear trout streams, thick forests, and endless solitude.

To continue the loop, retrace Highway 15 to the junction of Highway 35 and turn onto Highway 35. In just a few miles, Highway 35 passes Lake Roberts, a small lake set in pine-covered hills. A store, a small motel, a number of vacation homes, and Forest Service campgrounds line the shore. Anglers and boaters use the lake.

Beyond Lake Roberts, the road climbs gradually up a broad valley to the Continental Divide. Just past the divide, Highway 61 goes north. This gravel road leads into more of the Gila country and is very scenic. It's well worth a side trip, but some portions of this road generally require a high-clearance vehicle. It's also a great place for solitude. A sign at the start says NO FOOD, LODGING, OR GASOLINE NEXT 120 MILES. Believe it. See Drive 31.

After the Highway 61 junction, the highway gradually descends down the Mimbres River Valley. The road passes a small store and restaurant or two, a Forest Service ranger station, and a number of homes in the broad valley. In fall apples weigh down the trees in the many orchards lining the road. Horses and cattle graze in the green pastures. Near the old village of San Lorenzo, Highway 35 intersects Highway 152. Turn right on Highway 152 toward Silver City and Central.

The road climbs over a low arm of the Pinos Altos Range. Piñon pines and junipers dot the slopes. The highway passes the enormous open pit mine at Santa Rita. Be sure to stop and view the massive excavation. Giant dump trucks roar up out of the pit, carrying ore to the mill day and night. Greenish streaks on the walls of the pit indicate the copper ore. At Central, the highway ends at US 180. Turn right and drive the remaining 7 miles back to Silver City.

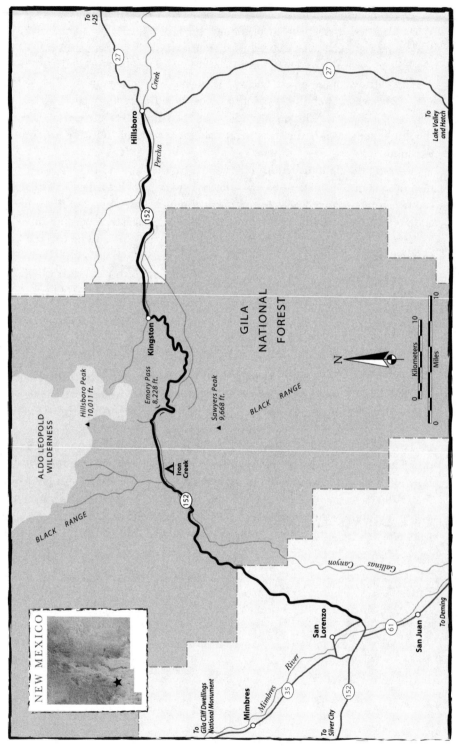

NEW MEXICO

To I-25

27

Creek

Hillsboro

27

To Lake Valley and Hatch

Percha

152

ALDO LEOPOLD WILDERNESS

Hillsboro Peak 10,011 ft. ▲

Kingston

Emory Pass 8,228 ft.

Sawyers Peak ▲ 9,668 ft.

GILA NATIONAL FOREST

BLACK RANGE

BLACK RANGE

Iron Creek

152

Gallinas Canyon

N

Kilometers 10
0

Miles 10
0

To Gila Cliff Dwellings National Monument

Mimbres

Mimbres River

35

San Lorenzo

152

61

San Juan

To Deming

To Silver City

23

Kingston–Hillsboro Ghost Towns

SAN LORENZO TO HILLSBORO

GENERAL DESCRIPTION: A 34-mile paved highway over the crest of the rugged Black Range and through two former ghost towns.

SPECIAL ATTRACTIONS: Former ghost towns of Kingston and Hillsboro, Aldo Leopold Wilderness, Gila National Forest, hiking, camping, views, fall color.

LOCATION: Southwestern New Mexico. The drive begins in San Lorenzo, a small town about 25 miles east of Silver City.

DRIVE ROUTE NUMBER: Highway 152.

TRAVEL SEASON: Year-round. The high mountain drive is cool and pleasant in summer, especially in late summer when thunderstorms have turned the mountains green. The route can also be beautiful in fall with colorful cottonwoods and aspens. The road

is spectacular in winter, but snow may temporarily require the use of snow tires or chains.

CAMPING: The USDA Forest Service maintains attractive Iron Creek Campground along the route. The Forest Service allows primitive camping in most other areas of the forest.

SERVICES: Limited food and lodging are available in Hillsboro and Kingston. Food is available in San Lorenzo. Gas is available in the Mimbres Valley near San Lorenzo. All services are available in nearby Silver City.

NEARBY ATTRACTIONS: City of Rocks State Park, Gila Wilderness, Gila Cliff Dwellings National Monument, Santa Rita open pit mine.

THE DRIVE

Highway 152 winds its way up and over the Black Range, via Emory Pass, and down to the old mining towns of Kingston and Hillsboro. The Black Range is a long, north–south mountain range with a crest that reaches elevations higher than 10,000 feet. The heavily forested mountains are rugged and remote. The 202,000-acre **Aldo Leopold Wilderness** occupies the heart of the range. Highway 152 is the only easy-access point to this mountainous high country. It is a steep, winding mountain road. Take it slow and enjoy the scenery.

The drive starts in **San Lorenzo,** a small village in the Mimbres River Valley. The Mimbres River gets its start high in the peaks of the Black Range. In the vicinity of San Lorenzo, it has carved a broad valley. In fall apples weigh down branches of trees in many orchards. Autumn also brings brilliant color changes to the cottonwoods and apple trees of the valley.

The area is famous as the home of the Mimbres people of the prehistoric Mogollon culture from about A.D. 1000 to A.D. 1250. Ruins of their pueblos are scattered across the valley and other nearby areas. The Mimbres people are famous for their pottery with its intricate black-on-white painted designs. The artists created elaborate geometric patterns and stylized human and animal figures. Little other prehistoric pottery from the Southwest can compare in craftsmanship.

San Lorenzo is a small agricultural village centered just off of Highway 152. It was founded by the Spaniards in 1714. From San Lorenzo, the highway immediately begins climbing into the foothills of the Black Range. At first, it passes open country with scattered piñon, juniper, and oak trees that dot the hillsides. Soon it enters the Gila National Forest. As the road climbs, the forest becomes thicker and tall ponderosa pines appear. The highway passes numerous marked trailheads, making the drive a hiker's paradise. The road drops down into the rocky gorge of Gallinas Canyon before resuming its climb. At least a trickle of water usually runs down the canyon. Pines, Douglas firs, cherry trees, and other species crowd the lush, narrow canyon bottom. Several primitive camp areas line the creek.

After a short distance, the highway turns up a tributary, Iron Creek, and passes a campground named after it. After a few more miles and many sharp curves, the highway reaches the crest at 8,228-foot Emory Pass. Be sure to stop at the marked Emory Pass Vista. The view stretches for miles to the east, all the way across the Rio Grande Valley. On a clear day, you may even be able to pick out 12,003-foot Sierra Blanca Peak 120 miles away in the Sacramento Mountains.

RECOMMENDED TRAILS

Two excellent trails start from the pass. One climbs up the crest to the north to 10,011-foot Hillsboro Peak. The peak has a fire lookout and tremendous views of much of southwestern New Mexico. Many other trails continue on into the Aldo Leopold Wilderness. The vast wilderness area was named in honor of Leopold, who first urged creation of areas that would be left undeveloped by man. He was instrumental in establishment of the nearby Gila Wilderness Area in 1924, the nation's first.

Another trail leads south from the pass to 9,668-foot Sawyer Peak. The trail climbs through a lush forest dominated by Douglas fir, ponderosa pine, and aspen to the wooded summit.

From Emory Pass, the highway drops rapidly down to **Kingston.** Silver was discovered near Kingston in 1880, and the town boomed overnight. As ore poured from the mines, the population skyrocketed to more than 7,000 people. Millions of dollars of silver fueled the prosperity. The liquor flowed freely in the town's twenty-two saloons. Gambling halls flourished, and prostitutes plied their trade at brothels on "Virtue Avenue." By the turn of the twentieth century, the town was dying. Ore bodies were exhausted and silver prices had crashed. Today, only a few scattered homes and businesses are tucked in the pines, a tiny remnant of the town's former

Fall aspens in the Aldo Leopold Wilderness

glory. During its heyday in the nineteenth century, Kingston was the richest silver producer in New Mexico. Today, the sleepy little town caters to artists and tourists.

A few miles down the highway in the foothills of the mountains lies **Hillsboro.** Like Kingston, it was a roaring mining town in the late nineteenth century. In 1877 gold was discovered and the rush was on. The town boomed and gold poured out of the mines. But, like Kingston, the mines ran dry, and the town declined after the turn of the century, nearly reaching ghost town status.

Today, artists and retirees have settled in Hillsboro, bringing new life to the former boomtown. The highway, which doubles as the main street, is a tree-shaded avenue lined with a small number of homes and businesses. Both Kingston and Hillsboro have bed-and-breakfast-type establishments, along with a few shops and cafes.

The **Black Range Museum** in Hillsboro describes the area's history and displays mementos of the mining period. It also contains some of Sadie Orchard's personal items. She operated brothels in Hillsboro and Kingston, along with respectable businesses. She lived in Hillsboro until her death in 1943. Every Labor Day weekend, the Apple Festival attracts many visitors to Hillsboro. Although the crowds are much more peaceful, they bring to mind the boom days when thousands of people lived in Hillsboro and Kingston.

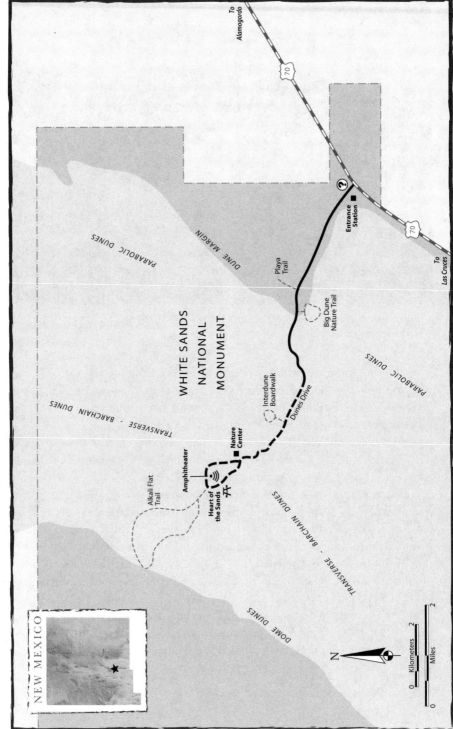

24

Heart of the Sands Drive

WHITE SANDS

GENERAL DESCRIPTION: A short 8-mile drive through part of the largest gypsum dune field in the world.

SPECIAL ATTRACTIONS: White Sands National Monument, hiking, sand-skiing.

LOCATION: South-central New Mexico. The drive begins at the entrance of White Sands National Monument, about 15 miles southwest of Alamogordo along U.S. Highway 70.

DRIVE ROUTE NAME: Heart of the Sands Drive.

TRAVEL SEASON: Year-round. The dunes can be very hot in summer but are still worth visiting in early morning or late afternoon. Occasional sandstorms, most common in spring, can make the drive temporarily unpleasant.

CAMPING: The monument has a primitive backcountry campsite that can be reached only by a short hike. The nearest public campgrounds are at Oliver Lee Memorial State Park south of Alamogordo, in the Lincoln National Forest in the Sacramento Mountains above Alamogordo, and at Aguirre Springs in the Organ Mountains near Las Cruces.

SERVICES: All services are located in nearby Alamogordo.

NEARBY ATTRACTIONS: Sacramento Mountains, Lincoln National Forest, Ski Apache and Ski Cloudcroft ski areas.

THE DRIVE

White Sands National Monument occupies only part of a vast sea of gypsum dunes that blanket part of the flat Tularosa Valley. Two hundred million years ago, shallow bays and lagoons covered much of southeastern New Mexico. The seawater contained dissolved gypsum, along with salt and other minerals. At times these bodies of water were cut off from the main ocean and evaporation accelerated, depositing a thick bed of gypsum-bearing rock called the Yeso Formation. Not surprisingly, *yeso* is the Spanish word for gypsum. The Permian seas created other sedimentary rocks, such as limestone and shale, that buried the Yeso Formation. About seventy million years ago, a large area around White Sands National Monument was uplifted in a large dome. Long north-south faults caused the center section of the dome to sink several thousand feet, forming a valley 100 miles long and 30 miles wide known as the Tularosa Basin. The basin is closed, with no outlet to the sea.

Dunes at the White Sands National Monument

On each side of the basin, the Sacramento and San Andres Mountains remained uplifted, their sheer cliffs exposing the ancient sedimentary rock layers.

Unlike the basin, the dunes at **White Sands** formed within only the last 25,000 years. During the wetter ice-age times of the Pleistocene, much of the Tularosa Basin was filled by a large body of water known as Lake Otero. Rain and snow falling on the Sacramento and San Andres Mountains washed over exposed sedimentary beds and dissolved gypsum. The gypsum-bearing water flowed into Lake Otero or sank down to the water table.

The climate became hotter and dryer, shrinking the lake and leaving only a small seasonal remnant, Lake Lucero, at a low point in the basin. As the lake water evaporated, gypsum came out of solution and was deposited on the bottom. Beneath the old lake bed, the ground water is still saturated with gypsum and other minerals. These saturated waters create large gypsum crystals of selenite that erosion exposes to the surface along the shores of Lake Lucero. The crystals deteriorate over time, adding to the supply of gypsum sand.

In spring strong southwest winds break the soft gypsum deposits and crystals into sand particles and dust. The wind carries the dust away and pushes the sand into dunes. The dunes have formed a large field to the northeast of the gypsum source at Lake Lucero and adjoining Alkali Flat. Covering 275 square miles, it is the largest dune field composed of gypsum in the world.

DUNE TRAILS

The drive starts at the visitor center, at the park entrance along US 70. Initially, it crosses desert flats but soon enters the dune field. A parking lot at the edge of the dune field is the trailhead for the easy, 1-mile Big Dune Trail. The marked nature trail meanders through the dunes and explains the natural history of White Sands.

A short distance into the dunes, the pavement ends, but the packed sand road surface is excellent for any vehicle. On the left, a small parking area marks the trailhead to the primitive camp area. If you have time and the weather is good, consider camping there on a full moon night. The white dunes form an eerie landscape in the bright moonlight.

As you progress farther into the monument, the dunes become larger and more closely spaced. At the short loop in **Heart of the Sands** at the end of the road, vegetation has almost disappeared, smothered under the shifting dunes. Picnic shelters are scattered along the loop. Kids, and some adults, run wild here, climbing the dunes and sliding, skiing, or rolling down the steep dune faces. Resign yourself to cleaning sand out of clothes and car and join the fun.

You may see film crews at work during your visit. Movie crews love the stark white landscape and average forty or fifty visits annually. Everything from feature-length movies, such as *White Sands*, to Eveready Bunny ads have been filmed here.

If you hike far out into the dune field, be careful not to get lost. Don't count on using your tracks to lead you back. Wind and tracks of other people will erase your footprints. Use the distant mountains as landmarks.

LEGEND OF THE DUNES

Try to stay until sunset. The last light turns the dunes gold and pink before the sun sinks below the serrated crest of the San Andres Mountains to the west. As the colors fade from the sky, an evening breeze may gust across the silent dunes, whirling wraithlike eddies of sand into the air. Pavla Blanca, the ghost of White Sands, haunts the dunes once more, searching for her lost love.

Legend says that in 1540 Hernando de Luna, a Spanish conquistador, set out with the expedition of Francisco Vasquez de Coronado to find the seven golden cities of Cibola. Luna left behind his betrothed, the beautiful Manuela, in Mexico City. The expedition crisscrossed the Southwest, hunting for rumored treasures and enduring great hardship. Apaches ambushed the party on the edge of the dunes, forcing the survivors to flee back to Mexico City. Luna was severely wounded and died somewhere in the shifting sands. Upon hearing of his death, Manuela set out to find her beloved and was never seen again.

According to the story, the ghost of the Spanish maiden still comes nightly to White Sands, seeking her lost lover buried somewhere beneath the endless dunes. The eddies of sand swirling across the dunes at dusk are the skirts of Manuela's long white wedding gown. Look carefully and maybe you will see Pavla Blanca, the ghost of Manuela.

Cloudcroft

ALAMOGORDO TO CLOUDCROFT

GENERAL DESCRIPTION: A 20-mile paved highway that climbs from the Tularosa Basin desert to the lush forests of the Sacramento Mountains.

SPECIAL ATTRACTIONS: Sacramento Mountains, Lincoln National Forest, New Mexico Museum of Space History, Ski Cloudcroft Ski Area, historic railroad, views, hiking, camping, fall color, cross-country skiing, mountain biking.

LOCATION: Southeastern New Mexico. The drive starts in Alamogordo.

DRIVE ROUTE NUMBER: U.S. Highway 70/54, U.S. Highway 82.

TRAVEL SEASON: Year-round. The drive is

cool and pleasant in summer. Aspens, cottonwoods, and apple trees make the drive very beautiful in late September and early October. Snows can necessitate the use of chains or snow tires at times in the winter, particularly near Cloudcroft.

CAMPING: The US Forest Service maintains several popular campgrounds in the cool forest near Cloudcroft.

SERVICES: All services are available in Alamogordo and Cloudcroft.

NEARBY ATTRACTIONS: White Sands National Monument, Ski Apache, Three Rivers Petroglyph Site, National Solar Observatory, Oliver Lee Memorial State Park.

THE DRIVE

The west flank of the **Sacramento Mountains** above Alamogordo is a towering wall of cliffs and steep slopes. The mountains rise a vertical mile from the Tularosa Valley floor to mountain summits south of Cloudcroft. The road from Alamogordo to Cloudcroft rises 4,300 feet, as noted in warning signs to truckers. The highway rapidly climbs through several life zones, from creosote bush and cacti at the bottom to spruce, fir, and aspen at Cloudcroft.

Start the drive in **Alamogordo,** a sprawling town of about 30,000 people located in the large, flat Tularosa Valley. The town got its start at the turn of the twentieth century when the El Paso and Northeastern Railroad was built through the Tularosa Valley. Its name means "large cottonwood."

Ranching, trade, and lumber were Alamogordo's primary businesses until World War II, when an air base was established to train bomber crews. The air base eventually became Holloman Air Force Base. White Sands Missile Range was created to test missiles and other weaponry in the vast Tularosa Valley. The military detonated the world's first atomic bomb at the Trinity Site on the missile range north of the town. NASA also maintains facilities in the valley, including an alternate landing site for the space shuttle.

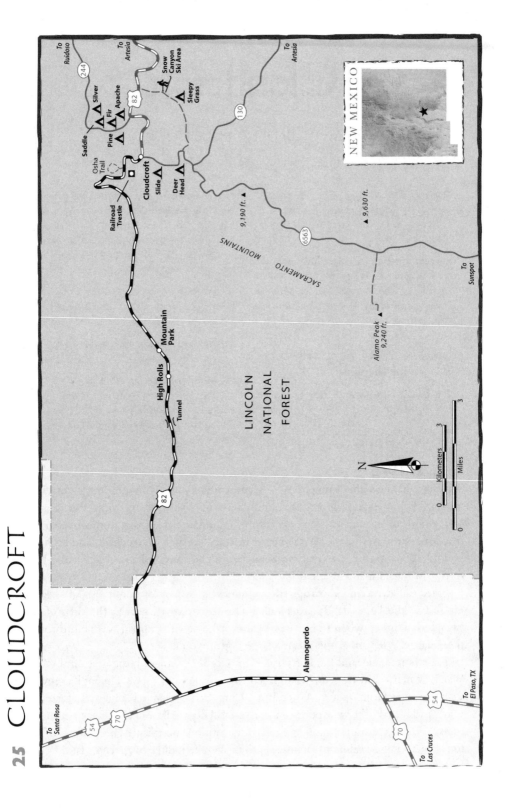

The city boomed with the government activities and is still largely dependent on them today. However, the creation of the sprawling military ranges meant eviction of many ranchers from their property. One rancher in particular, John Prather, resisted all efforts to remove him. His story inspired Edward Abbey's novel *Fire on the Mountain*. Even today, some bitterness lingers in the Tularosa Valley.

The **New Mexico Museum of Space History** describes human activities in space. It houses rocket engines, satellites, missiles, moon rocks, and many other space-oriented items. A planetarium and theater with an impressive wrap-around screen are added attractions.

MOUNTAIN DRIVE

Drive north of Alamogordo on US 70/54 about 3 miles to the junction with US 82 on the right. Follow US 82 to Cloudcroft. Within a mile, it abruptly begins climbing into the mountains. The very steep west face of the Sacramento Mountains was created by a huge fault. Another parallel fault on the west side of the Tularosa Valley shifted at the same time, causing a large block of the earth's crust to sink and create the valley. The rocks in the cliffs towering over Alamogordo match those exposed in cliffs of the San Andres Mountains far across the valley to the west.

The highway climbs quickly, leaving the desert behind. Juniper and piñon pine trees soon dot the hills. The highway climbs up the steep south wall of deep Fresnal Canyon and enters a tunnel, a rarity in New Mexico. Plan to stop at the overlook just before the tunnel. A cottonwood-lined stream tumbles down the canyon bottom far below. Views extend many miles to the west across the Tularosa Valley.

About a mile after the tunnel, the highway leaves the canyon and enters the mountain village of High Rolls. The small village and the adjoining town of Mountain Park occupy a relatively level bench on the overall steep west slope of the Sacramento Mountains. Thick piñon and juniper trees blanket the hills, and cottonwoods line the creek bottoms. Apple trees and other fruits and vegetables thrive in the cooler, moister climate of the two towns. Roadside stands offer produce for sale, particularly in early fall when the apples ripen.

After leaving Mountain Park, US 82 begins climbing steeply again. The forest becomes more lush, first with ponderosa pine, then with Douglas fir, blue spruce, and aspen, colorful in fall. Just before reaching Cloudcroft, a large old trestle appears below the highway to the right. The massive wooden structure is a remnant of the old logging railroad that once wound its way through much of the Sacramento Mountains around Cloudcroft. Stop at the large pull-out to view it. The trestle is tall, and probably not structurally sound. Do not risk climbing on it.

The Osha Trail begins at a pull-out just across the road from the trestle. The 2.5-mile loop trail is steep for the first quarter mile but is then quite easy. The path provides great views of White Sands and the Tularosa Valley far below, plus passes through lush forest and mountain meadows. Maples and aspens along the trail can make the walk especially worthwhile in the fall.

Historic Mexican Canyon railroad trestle

The Lodge at Cloudcroft

CLOUDCROFT

The drive ends at the rustic mountain town of Cloudcroft less than a mile from the trestle and the Osha Trail. Cloudcroft was founded in 1899 as a logging town to provide ties for the El Paso and Northeastern Railroad being built in the Tularosa Valley. A spur line, known as the Cloud Climbing Railroad, was built into the mountains to Cloudcroft. From the town, a network of tracks was built into the forest to harvest timber. The trestle along US 82 is one of the most prominent remnants of the railroad.

People from El Paso wishing to escape the summer heat quickly discovered Cloudcroft. A lodge built in 1899 to house construction workers became a tourist resort. The lodge burned in 1909 but was rebuilt in its elaborate present-day incarnation. The railroad is gone, but the lodge still caters to tourists. At over 9,200 feet, its golf course is one of the highest in the world. Watch for bears as you stroll down the grassy fairways tucked into the lush forest. Legend has it that the ghost of Rebecca, a flirtatious chambermaid killed by a jealous lover, haunts the lodge.

Cloudcroft makes a good base for exploring the surrounding country. The sprawling **Lincoln National Forest** provides opportunities for hiking, camping, skiing, horseback riding, fall color viewing, and other outdoor activities. Drives 26, 27, and 28 describe three of many possible mountain drives in the Sacramento Mountains. Cloudcroft provides an excellent escape from the desert heat of southern New Mexico and West Texas in summer, just as it did more than one hundred years ago.

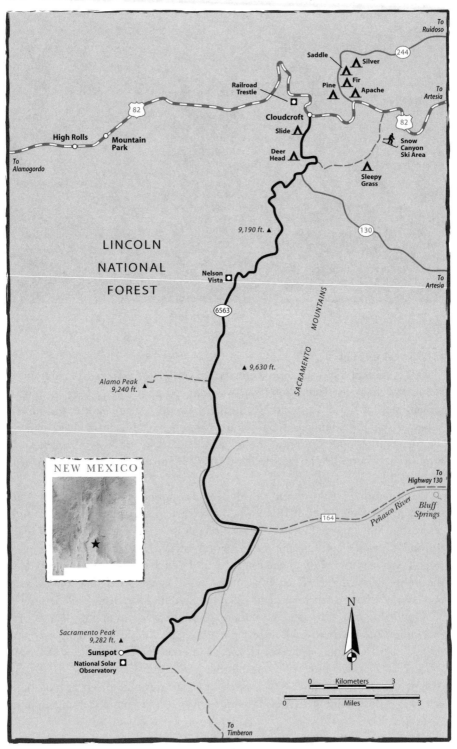

To Ruidoso

244

Saddle

Silver

Railroad Trestle

Pine

Fir

Apache

82

To Artesia

Cloudcroft

82

High Rolls

Mountain Park

Slide

Snow Canyon Ski Area

To Alamogordo

Deer Head

Sleepy Grass

9,190 ft.

130

To Artesia

LINCOLN

NATIONAL

Nelson Vista

FOREST

6563

SACRAMENTO MOUNTAINS

▲ 9,630 ft.

Alamo Peak 9,240 ft. ▲

NEW MEXICO

To Highway 130

Peñasco River

Bluff Springs

164

N

Sacramento Peak 9,282 ft. ▲

Sunspot

National Solar Observatory

0 Kilometers 3

0 Miles 3

To Timberon

Sunspot Scenic Byway

CLOUDCROFT TO SUNSPOT

GENERAL DESCRIPTION: A 17-mile paved highway that winds through miles of lush mountain forest to the large observatory complex at Sunspot.

SPECIAL ATTRACTIONS: Sacramento Mountains, Lincoln National Forest, National Solar Observatory, hiking, camping, mountain biking, cross-country skiing, fall color.

LOCATION: Southeastern New Mexico. The drive starts in Cloudcroft.

DRIVE ROUTE NUMBER: Highway 130, Highway 6563.

TRAVEL SEASON: Year-round. The drive is pleasant and cool in summer. Fall color can

be spectacular. The high mountain route is plowed in winter but is often icy and snow-packed. Chains or snow tires may be necessary at those times.

CAMPING: The Lincoln National Forest maintains campgrounds along the route at Deer Head and Sleepy Grass. Primitive camping is allowed throughout most of the rest of the forest.

SERVICES: All services are available in Cloudcroft.

NEARBY ATTRACTIONS: Ski Apache and Ski Cloudcroft ski areas, White Sands National Monument, Three Rivers Petroglyph Site, Oliver Lee Memorial State Park.

THE DRIVE

The drive from Cloudcroft to Sunspot winds through miles of lush forest of pine, Douglas fir, aspen, blue spruce, and other trees. It ends at one of the world's premier solar observatories.

The drive starts in **Cloudcroft,** a small mountain town founded in 1899 as a logging center for the El Paso and Northeastern Railroad. Follow Highway 130 south out of town. In about a mile the road passes popular Deer Head Campground on the right and the turnoff to Sleepy Grass Campground on the left. A short distance beyond the campgrounds lies the junction of Highway 130 and Highway 6563, the official start of the scenic byway. Highway 130, a very scenic route in itself, continues east to Mayhill, but turn right on Highway 6563 for this drive description.

Before good roads were built in the Sacramento Mountains, a small logging railroad provided access to the forest. Quite a bit of Highway 6563 follows one of the old railroad routes. Unfortunately, recent road widening projects destroyed much of the evidence of the historic railroad. However, observant drivers can still see the railroad bed in places, along with a few rotting cross ties.

FALL COLOR VIEWS

This drive and other roads in the Cloudcroft area provide one of the best places in southern New Mexico to view the fall color change of the aspens. Sometime in late September, the first leaves turn yellow as the days shorten and the nights become chilly. Soon, whole hillsides are painted gold by the changing trees. Oddly, on any one mountainside, a grove of aspens may still be green, another may be brilliant yellow, and a third may be leafless. Unlike many trees, aspens spread mostly through root suckers. Hence, an entire grove may be clones, in effect the same tree with identical genes, so naturally the grove turns color at the same time.

Less than a quarter mile after the start of Highway 6563, the marked **Rim Trail** begins on the right side of the road at the entrance to the Slide (Group) Campground. The 14-mile **National Recreation Trail** parallels much of the highway to Sunspot. The trail has some ups and downs, but in general is quite easy as it follows the west rim of the mountains. There are multiple access points to the trail along Highway 6563 and side roads, so small portions of the trail can easily be hiked. Here and there, the trail gives good views of White Sands and the Tularosa Valley far below. Between miles 2 and 3, just past Haynes Canyon, the trail traverses a substantial grove of maples, beautiful in fall. Be sure to go left at the large trailhead sign, not down the gully to the right into Deer Head Campground.

The highway slowly winds south along the mountain crest. Unpaved forest roads disappear into the trees at regular intervals, inviting exploration. Many of these side roads are excellent for mountain bikes. In winter, when snow blankets the forest, these roads and open meadows attract cross-country skiers.

About 6 miles from Cloudcroft, the short **Nelson Vista Trail** starts on the right side of the road. The easy trail has interpretive signs about the forest, plus gives great views of White Sands and the Tularosa Valley.

The turnoff to Bluff Springs is on the left about 10 miles from Cloudcroft. The side road follows the Peñasco River downstream about 4 miles to the springs. The first 2 miles are paved; the last 2 are gravel. The springs bubble up from the base of a wooded mountainside, flow across a meadow, and pour over a travertine waterfall before flowing into the river. The railroad grade is particularly prominent at the springs. A small trestle still survives a short distance up the railroad bed from the waterfall. The old railroad beds make great hiking and mountain biking trails because of their gentle grade.

Three miles beyond the Bluff Springs turnoff, the Cathey Peak Vista provides more good views. Beyond Cathey Peak, a major forest road turns off to the Sacramento River, the resort community of Timberon, and many other forest destinations.

SOLAR OBSERVATORY

The highway then climbs the last bit to **Sunspot,** the small community at the **National Solar Observatory** on Sacramento Peak. Like all observatories, this one was located on a high mountain to lessen atmospheric interference with observa-

Mountain biker in the Sacramento Mountains

tions. However, unlike most observatories that are dedicated to observing stars, planets, galaxies, and other dim objects, this site concentrates on the sun. Astronomers here attempt to learn more about basic solar structures and processes and their effect on the earth. The observatory also provides information to other organizations, helping determine the sun's effect on radio communications, spaceflight, and satellite operations.

The observatory offers an interesting self-guided tour of the facilities. The short walk first passes the Grain Bin Dome, the observatory's first facility, built in a modest Sears Roebuck grain bin. Probably the most interesting instrument is the Vacuum Tower Telescope housed in an oddly shaped, thirteen-story-tall white tower. Although the building and its instruments are impressive, unseen components are even more so. Like an iceberg, most of the telescope is hidden in a 220-foot-deep pit under the building. Astronomers designed the tower telescope to observe tiny features of the sun. The resolving power, or ability to see detail in small objects, of the telescope is excellent, the equivalent of reading a license plate from 60 miles away.

The observatory offers more elaborate guided tours on Friday, Saturday, and Sunday in the summer. Sunspot lies at over 9,200 feet, so don't try to run up and down the hills unless you're acclimated. Also, lightning is common on this mountaintop during storms. Be sure to visit the scenic viewpoint by the Tower Telescope before you leave. The desert below bakes under the New Mexico sun, while cool, pine-scented breezes make Sunspot an excellent summer destination.

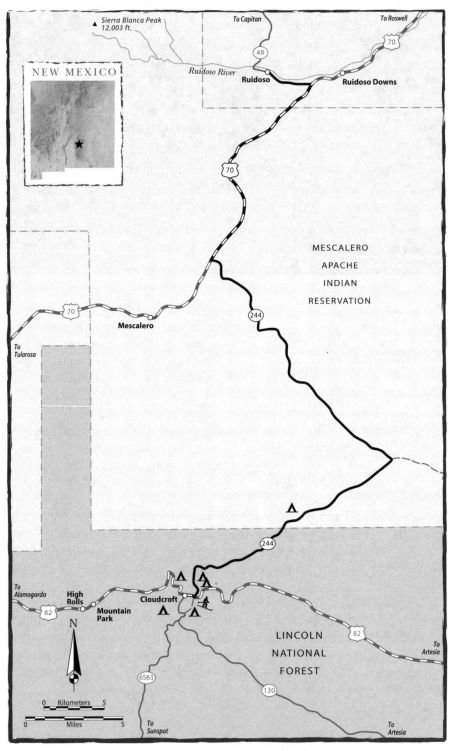

Sacramento Mountain Crest

CLOUDCROFT TO RUIDOSO

GENERAL DESCRIPTION: A 42-mile drive through the forested Sacramento Mountains between the resort towns of Cloudcroft and Ruidoso.

SPECIAL ATTRACTIONS: Sacramento Mountains, Lincoln National Forest, Mescalero Apache Indian Reservation, Ski Cloudcroft Ski Area, Ruidoso Downs, hiking, camping, cross-country skiing, mountain biking, fall color.

LOCATION: Southeastern New Mexico. The drive starts in Cloudcroft.

DRIVE ROUTE NUMBER: U.S. Highway 82, Highway 244, U.S. Highway 70.

TRAVEL SEASON: Year-round. The drive is cool and pleasant in summer. Aspens usually provide good fall color, especially on the first part of the drive. Heavy snow is common in winter; chains and snow tires may sometimes be required.

CAMPING: The Lincoln National Forest maintains several campgrounds on the first part of the route: Pine, Apache, Silver, and Saddle. Primitive camping is allowed in most of the rest of the national forest.

SERVICES: All services are available in Cloudcroft and Ruidoso.

NEARBY ATTRACTIONS: White Sands National Monument, Three Rivers Petroglyph Site, Ski Apache ski area, White Mountain Wilderness, Capitan Mountains Wilderness, Lincoln State Monument, Smokey Bear Historical State Park, Oliver Lee Memorial State Park.

THE DRIVE

The drive from Cloudcroft to Ruidoso is a cool summer escape from nearby desert cities such as Alamogordo, El Paso, Roswell, and Carlsbad. The road follows the crest of the Sacramento Mountains through the heart of the Mescalero Apache Indian Reservation.

A number of subranges compose the sprawling mass of the **Sacramento Mountains,** one of the largest mountain chains in New Mexico. To the east lie the broad, low Pecos River Valley and the start of the southern Great Plains. Travelers approaching from the east welcome the cool forested mountains after the endless, hot monotony of the plains.

Many people casually passing through New Mexico on interstate highways assume that the state is little more than hot desert, especially in the south. The lush

Sacramento Mountains quickly belie that notion. The mountains reach their high point at 12,003-foot Sierra Blanca Peak near Ruidoso. Only the Sangre de Cristo Mountains near Santa Fe and Taos are higher. Snow buries the mountains every winter, enough to support two downhill ski areas. Texans discovered the mountains long ago as a summer refuge from the heat and as a winter sports center. Cloudcroft and Ruidoso in particular often have more Texans in residence than New Mexicans.

The quiet drive starts in **Cloudcroft,** a rustic mountain village founded in 1899 as a logging town. Ruidoso is a much bigger and busier tourist center with major attractions such as Ruidoso Downs and Ski Apache ski area. Cloudcroft appeals to those seeking a quieter, more relaxed vacation.

FROM CLOUDCROFT TO MESCALERO

From Cloudcroft, head east on US 82 a little more than a mile to the Highway 244 junction. Turn left, or north, on Highway 244 toward Ruidoso. The road soon passes a concentration of Forest Service campgrounds tucked into lush woods of pine, fir, spruce, and aspen. The first few miles of this drive, and other areas south of Cloudcroft, are usually the best areas to see aspens in the fall. After passing Silver Campground, the highway slowly descends down Silver Springs Canyon. As the highway descends, it leaves behind most of the higher mountain trees such as the aspen. In a few miles, the highway leaves the Lincoln National Forest and enters the **Mescalero Apache Indian Reservation.** Ponderosa pines dominate most of the drive through the reservation.

The Mescalero Apache Reservation is a 460,000-acre tract of land in the heart of the Sacramento Mountains. It splits two large segments of the Lincoln National Forest, one centered around Cloudcroft and Sunspot, the other centered around Ruidoso and Capitan. The Mescalero Apaches once dominated the mountainous areas of southeastern New Mexico. Not surprisingly, they resisted displacement by Anglo and Hispanic settlers. Many battles were fought between the Apaches and U.S. troops in and around the Sacramento Mountains. Today the tribe is one of the most prosperous in the country. They operate the large and popular Ski Apache downhill ski area on the slopes of Sierra Blanca Peak as well as manage logging and grazing industries in the forest. Their Inn of the Mountain Gods is a premier resort tucked into the pines lining Lake Mescalero. The resort offers golf, tennis, gambling, horseback riding, and many other activities. To enter other areas of the reservation, permission must be obtained from the tribe in Mescalero.

A short distance into the reservation is the Silver Lake Campground on the left. The Apache tribe operates a small trout fishing lake and campground here.

After passing through about 30 miles of forest out from Cloudcroft, the drive intersects US 70. Unlike Highway 244, US 70 is a busy, although still scenic, four-lane highway. Turn right on US 70 and join the throngs heading to Ruidoso from El Paso and Las Cruces.

Old barns on the Mescalero Apache Indian Reservation

PEAK VIEWS

The divided highway climbs steadily to a high point at Apache Summit. On the way down the other side of the pass, a grand view opens up of Sierra Blanca Peak. The peak towers over the surrounding mountains, dominating the landscape. A marker at a pull-out on the right tells about the mountain. Because of its 12,003-foot elevation, the peak is snowcapped much of the year. Not surprisingly, Sierra Blanca means "white mountain" in Spanish.

Soon the drive ends in the bustling resort town of **Ruidoso.** Motels, cabins, and vacation homes line the Ruidoso River canyon bottom, and condos cling to the pine-covered hills above. Ruidoso was founded in the late nineteenth century as Dowlin's Mill. The settlement's name was soon changed to Ruidoso, which means "noisy," because of the creek that tumbles down the canyon. The gristmill still stands as a gift shop and even grinds flour.

People wishing to escape the summer heat of the desert flatlands discovered Ruidoso after the turn of the twentieth century. After World War II, the town boomed and has been growing ever since. A large horse-racing track, **Ruidoso Downs,** was built in the valley and attracted further development. Every summer, quarter horses pound the circular track, racing for prizes and fueling bets by eager fans. On Labor Day, prizes of $2.5 million attract keen competition in the world's richest quarter horse race, the All American Futurity.

Like Cloudcroft, Ruidoso makes a fine central point from which to explore the surrounding country. Hike along the forest ridges of the White Mountain Wilderness or ski down the snowy slopes of Sierra Blanca Peak. Discover the birthplace of Smokey Bear in Capitan and learn about Billy the Kid's involvement in the Lincoln County Wars in Lincoln. Or just relax in the cool pines and put off your return to the heat and crowds of the city as long as possible.

Sierra Blanca Peak

ALTO TO SKI APACHE

GENERAL DESCRIPTION: A 12-mile paved highway that climbs up the highest mountain in southern New Mexico to Ski Apache ski area.

SPECIAL ATTRACTIONS: Sierra Blanca Peak, Ski Apache, Lincoln National Forest, White Mountain Wilderness, hiking, camping, views, fall color.

LOCATION: Southeastern New Mexico. The drive starts at the junction of Highway 48 and Highway 532 in Alto about 5 miles north of Ruidoso.

DRIVE ROUTE NUMBER: Highway 532.

TRAVEL SEASON: Year-round. The drive is pleasant and cool during hot summer days. Fall color can be spectacular. Because of the

ski area, the road is plowed in winter. However, the road can be treacherous, requiring the use of chains and snow tires.

CAMPING: The Lincoln National Forest maintains a campground at Oak Grove along the route and several others nearby. Primitive camping is allowed throughout most of the national forest.

SERVICES: All services are available in Alto and nearby Ruidoso.

NEARBY ATTRACTIONS: Lincoln State Monument, Valley of Fires Recreation Area, Smokey Bear Historical State Park, Ruidoso Downs, Ski Cloudcroft ski area, Capitan Mountains Wilderness, Three Rivers Petroglyph Site, ghost town of White Oaks.

THE DRIVE

The drive up to Ski Apache is one of the highest and most spectacular in the state. The ski area is on the upper slopes of 12,003-foot Sierra Blanca Peak, the highest mountain in southern New Mexico. The mountain, snowcapped for much of the year, surprises many first time visitors to southern New Mexico who come expecting desert.

The peak is high enough to reach above timberline; its summit is bare of trees. Alpine wildflowers blanket the upper slopes in summer. Believe it or not, glaciers covered the peak in past ice ages. A small glacial cirque is visible from Windy Point, along the drive. Snow often remains on the peak well into summer. It's not surprising that Texans flock to the area to escape the summer heat.

The drive starts in **Alto**, a small resort town a little north of Ruidoso. The route, although paved, is steep and winding and may be difficult for large recreation vehicles. Highway 532 follows Eagle Creek upstream at a relatively gentle grade. The junction with Forest Road 117 is on the right. The gravel side road leads to Monjeau Lookout and Skyline Campground. The fire lookout gives great views of the mountains and has several trailheads for the White Mountain Wilderness.

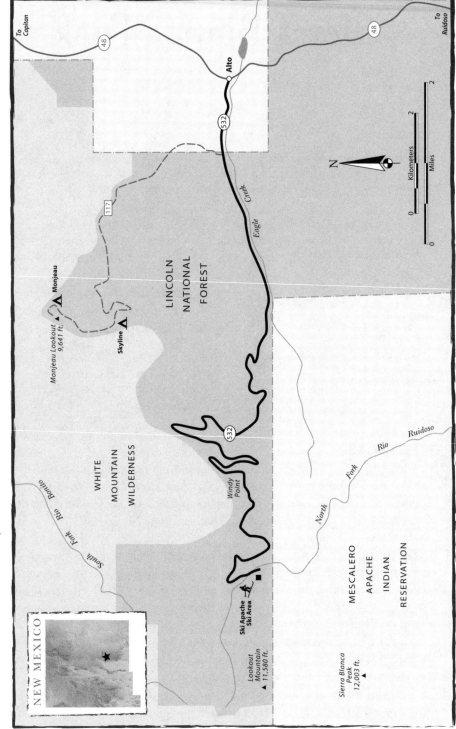

After about 3 miles, the highway leaves Eagle Creek and begins climbing in earnest. Oak Grove Campground lies on the right, on a ridgetop. After passing Oak Grove, the road begins a series of large switchbacks up the mountain. Broad views open up to the east, but if you're driving, you'll be too busy negotiating the road to notice. After several hairpin turns, the road reaches Windy Point Vista at about 10,000 feet. Pull into the parking lot carefully; it's on a blind curve.

The view stretches for miles. The towns of Ruidoso and Alto are visible below. To the south, the Sacramento Mountains stretch to Cloudcroft and beyond. The Pecos River Valley and the Great Plains lie far to the east. Sierra Blanca Peak towers into the sky just to the west.

BIRTHPLACE OF AN ICON

To the northeast, the **Capitan Mountains** rise into the sky. Smokey Bear was born there. After a devastating forest fire in 1950, a black bear cub was found clinging to a burned pine. The young bear was treated for his burns and became the living symbol of the USDA Forest Service's fire prevention campaign. He died in 1976 after living a long life at the National Zoo in Washington, D.C.

The 10,000-foot Capitan Mountains are a rarity in the United States—they trend east-west, rather than north-south as is much more common. Like Sierra Blanca Peak, they are part of the large chain of mountains known as the Sacramentos. Unlike the area around Ruidoso, which is thronged with vacationers, the rugged Capitan Mountains are virtually devoid of people. The 35,822-acre Capitan Mountains Wilderness attracts hikers seeking a quiet escape from civilization.

The historic town of **Lincoln** rests on a bank of the Rio Bonito on the south side of the Capitan Mountains. Today the sleepy little village gives no hint of the violent Lincoln County War. Late in the nineteenth century, the area developed into prosperous cattle ranching country. Nearby Fort Stanton purchased large quantities of beef to feed soldiers and reservation Apaches. Keen competition developed between merchants to supply area ranchers and farmers. For some time Lawrence Murphy owned the only store and was able to charge monopoly prices. To maintain his political and economic power, Murphy was ruthless.

WAR IN LINCOLN

Alexander McSween and an Englishman, John Tunstall, opened a store to compete with Murphy. The war started February 18, 1878, when gunmen hired by Murphy and his allies murdered Tunstall. Murphy controlled the sheriff and, in fact, the sheriff then deputized the murderers as a posse to find the murderers.

Friends and allies of Tunstall and McSween formed a group that called themselves the "Regulators" to avenge Tunstall's murder. One member of the group was William Bonney, also known as Billy the Kid. Soon enough, the Regulators killed two members of the posse that had murdered Tunstall. Shortly thereafter, the group ambushed the sheriff, killing him and one of his deputies.

The violence escalated with more killings. The territorial governor appealed to President Rutherford B. Hayes to send federal troops to help quell the fighting. Fort Stanton soldiers were sent but did little more than observe for a time and then withdraw. The McSween-Tunstall forces were popular with area ranchers and farmers after having suffered from the poor business practices of Murphy.

The war culminated in a battle in July when McSween and his allies holed up in his house. After five days, the house was torched. McSween stepped outside to surrender but was shot dead. A deputy and two of McSween's supporters were also killed in the battle. Billy the Kid and the other Regulators escaped into darkness from the burning house.

The uproar over the violence led President Hayes to replace the territorial governor with Lew Wallace. To end the warfare, Wallace offered an amnesty in November to all participants of the Lincoln County War, except Billy the Kid. However, the governor was anxious to settle the problem in Lincoln and promised to protect the Kid from prosecution. The Kid submitted to arrest and agreed to testify. However, the men against whom he was to testify escaped from jail. Billy the Kid left town, prompting the governor to post a reward for his capture. Pat Garrett caught up with him in December 1880 and arrested him.

The next April, Billy the Kid was sentenced to death for the murder of Sheriff Brady and taken to Lincoln for execution, even though the governor had promised him protection. Aided by friends, he escaped from the Lincoln County jail. Pat Garrett later killed him in Fort Sumner. Many books and movies chronicle the life and exploits of Billy the Kid. One of the best-known movies, *Young Guns*, dramatized the Lincoln County War.

Fortunately, visitors to Windy Point have little to fear from Billy the Kid or other outlaws. If lightning storms are around, however, the Point is not a healthy place to be.

TO SKI APACHE

From Windy Point, the highway contours along the mountainside through groves of aspen for about 2 miles and then drops down a short distance to the base of Ski Apache in the bottom of the north fork of the Rio Ruidoso. In late September and early October, the aspens can paint the mountains gold.

Lush forests of spruce and fir cloak the hillsides of the ski area. Several chair lifts and a gondola climb the slopes. Surprisingly, considering its location in southern New Mexico, **Ski Apache** has the largest skier capacity of any area in the state. It receives an average of more than 180 inches of snow every winter and has a vertical drop of about 1,800 feet. Not surprisingly, given its location in southeastern New Mexico, Ski Apache is very popular with Texans. It is operated by the Mescalero Apache Indian tribe, one of the most prosperous in the nation. Their reservation covers 460,000 acres of the Sacramento Mountains south of Ruidoso and includes the summit of Sierra Blanca Peak.

Aspens at Sierra Blanca

A popular trailhead for the **White Mountain Wilderness** lies along the highway on the right just before the ski area. Trails lead from there to Monjeau Lookout and the crest of the mountains. Other wilderness trails lead to old mines and rushing mountain streams filled with trout.

The views from the crest or from 11,580-foot Lookout Mountain at the top of the ski area are incredible. On a clear day, you can see much of southern and central New Mexico and even as far as West Texas. The hike to the summit of Sierra Blanca will leave you breathless but awed by the view. The summit does lie on the Mescalero Apache Reservation, however, so be sure to obtain permission from the tribe in Mescalero before you begin the ascent.

Don't wear out your brakes on the steep drive down the mountain. Use a low gear to slow your speed.

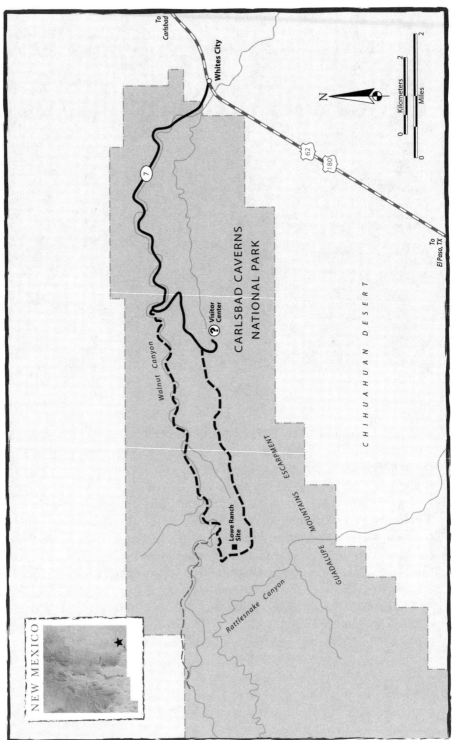

Carlsbad Caverns Highway & Scenic Loop

WHITES CITY TO CARLSBAD CAVERNS NATIONAL PARK

GENERAL DESCRIPTION: A 7-mile paved highway through the foothills of the Guadalupe Mountains to Carlsbad Cavern and a 9-mile gravel loop through the park backcountry.

SPECIAL ATTRACTIONS: Carlsbad Caverns National Park, Chihuahuan Desert, hiking, views.

LOCATION: Southeastern New Mexico. The drive starts in Whites City, a small tourist town about 20 miles southwest of Carlsbad.

DRIVE ROUTE NAME/NUMBER: Highway 7, Carlsbad Caverns Scenic Loop.

TRAVEL SEASON: Year-round. The drive can be hot in summer. The rest of the year, especially fall, is usually more pleasant. Although it can be hot, the park is green and most

attractive in late summer after the rains have arrived. Carlsbad Cavern itself remains a cool 56 degrees year-round.

CAMPING: Only primitive backcountry camping is allowed in the park. The nearest public campgrounds are in Guadalupe Mountains National Park and Brantley Dam State Park.

SERVICES: All services are available in Carlsbad and Whites City. Food is available at Carlsbad Caverns National Park.

NEARBY ATTRACTIONS: Guadalupe Mountains National Park, Lincoln National Forest, Sitting Bull Falls, Slaughter Canyon Cave (New Cave), Living Desert State Park, Brantley Dam State Park, President's Park.

THE DRIVE

Carlsbad Cavern is world famous as one of the largest caves in the world. One chamber, the Big Room, has 14 acres of floor space and a 255-feet-high ceiling. Immense stalactites and stalagmites grow from the ceiling and floor of the Big Room and many of the cavern's other chambers, dwarfing cavern visitors.

The drive starts in **Whites City,** a small town founded to provide services to Carlsbad Caverns National Park visitors. The town lies at the edge of the long ridge that makes up the Guadalupe Mountains. The mountains are a large, uplifted block that tilts upward to the south. Although most of the mountain range lies in New Mexico, the highest part of the triangular wedge lies in Texas. The Texas section of the mountains are high enough to be partly forested. Guadalupe Mountains National Park contains most of the Texas section, preserving a rugged landscape of towering cliffs, deep canyons, hidden oases, and the state's highest peak. Most of the mountains in New Mexico lie within **Carlsbad Caverns National Park** and the Lincoln National Forest.

The highway to Carlsbad Cavern enters the mountains abruptly at the edge of Whites City. For most of the 7-mile paved drive, the highway follows Walnut Canyon upstream. Except during floods, the canyon is dry, its floor dominated by white limestone cobbles and boulders. Small, scattered walnut trees give the canyon its name. Cliffs of weathered limestone make up the canyon walls and desert plants carpet the slopes.

DESERT LIFE

The park lies at the northern edge of the **Chihuahuan Desert** and has a dry climate. The Chihuahuan Desert's plant life sets it apart from other deserts. One plant in particular, the lechuguilla, is called an indicator plant for the Chihuahuan Desert; it lives nowhere else. Its leaves grow in a green rosette of thick, fibrous blades tipped with needle-sharp spines. The plants can grow into thick patches that are difficult to cross without spearing an ankle.

A lechuguilla blooms only once in its life. After building up a food supply for as much as ten or fifteen years, it quickly sends up a green asparagus-like stalk ten or more feet tall. After the stalk flowers, the entire plant dies, its food supply exhausted.

Several roadside pull-outs have exhibits that describe some of the natural and human history of the park. The highway begins its climb out of the canyon with a big horseshoe bend. Locals call the climb the Big Hill. Notice the heavy cut-stone guardrail on the downhill side of the road. It was built by the Civilian Conservation Corps during the Depression, as were many other park facilities. Water drips down one side of the road cut from a seep, or small spring. On the hill above, several bigtooth maples and other trees thrive with the extra moisture. Although Carlsbad Caverns National Park seems dry and desolate, hidden seeps and springs create small oases. Pull-outs partway up the hill and at the top on the rim provide excellent views of the canyon. Both of these pull-outs are on the other side of the road and are more easily and safely accessed when you come back down the highway.

After leaving the canyon, the road follows a gentle drainage and ridgetops to the highway's end at the large visitor center above the cave. Ignore several side roads that turn off the main highway. At the visitor center, you realize that the highway has climbed up to the top of the mountains. Views stretch far south into Texas on clear days, as far as the Davis Mountains more than 100 miles away. The entire eastern escarpment of the Guadalupe Mountains is visible, including the high peaks of Guadalupe Mountains National Park.

Be sure to take one of the cavern tours. The total length of the 3 miles of paved trails is very worthwhile, although shorter tours are available. The rounded desert hills give no hint of the wonders beneath your feet. More than 31 known miles of passages and rooms wind through the limestone heart of the mountains.

CREATING THE CAVERNS

More than 200 million years ago, an inland sea covered the area. At the edge of this sea, marine creatures created the massive Capitan Reef by depositing calcium carbonate, which later became limestone. The reef ringed much of the ancient sea and stretched far into West Texas. Eventually, the sea dried up and the reef was buried under thousands of feet of sediment. Later, faulting uplifted blocks of the reef in the Guadalupe, Glass, and Apache Mountains of West Texas and southeastern New Mexico.

Fractures in the rock gave rainwater a passage into the thick limestone beds. Carbon dioxide from the air made the water slightly acidic and allowed it to dissolve limestone and form underground chambers. Recent research indicates that another process was even more important to the formation of caves in the Guadalupe Mountains. The ancient seas that created the reef also deposited enormous quantities of organic matter. Over millions of years, heat and pressure converted this material into oil and gas. Today, petroleum production is a major industry in southeastern New Mexico and West Texas. Over time hydrogen sulfide gas escaped from oil and gas reservoirs near the mountains. It combined with oxygenated water, creating sulfuric acid. This strong acid is thought to have dissolved out many of the enormous underground chambers for which the Guadalupe Mountains are famous.

The tours descend more than 800 feet into Carlsbad Cavern. You can either walk down through the natural entrance or descend via elevators. If you have time and energy, I highly recommend that you take the tour through the natural entrance. Be sure to wear sturdy nonskid walking shoes or boots. Take a sweater; the cave remains a constant 56 degrees all year. Various tours visit different parts of the cave, some guided, some self-guided. Some, such as the natural entrance route, follow paved trails with electric lights; others are more primitive and require hard hats, hand-carried lights, climbing, and crawling.

As you would suspect, many other caves are hidden in the Guadalupe Mountains. The park service offers reservation-only trips through Slaughter Canyon Cave (formerly called New Cave) daily in the summer and on weekends the rest of the year. Steep, rocky dirt trails and lack of electric lights make the trip quite rugged. By using lanterns and flashlights, the tour gives a good feel of the experiences of early cave explorers. The park also offers strenuous, primitive tours of Spider Cave.

A major discovery in 1986 in Lechuguilla Cave has led to one of the biggest cave finds in recent history. Expeditions have pushed its known length to 112 miles, third longest in the United States and more than three times as long as Carlsbad Cavern. With a known depth of 1,604 feet, it is now the deepest limestone cave in the country. The cave has become very important to researchers in studies of cavern development but is not open to the public. Its remote wilderness location, extreme depth, multiple deep pits, and widely scattered delicate formations make commercial development of the cave impractical.

The Christmas Tree formation, Slaughter Canyon Cave, Carlsbad Caverns National Park

After you finish your cavern tour, continue with the rest of the drive. Backtrack down the highway from the visitor center about half a mile to a gravel road on the left, or west, side of the road. This 9-mile one-way loop is well maintained and passable by any vehicle, except possibly large recreation vehicles. A guide, keyed to numbered markers along the road, describes the natural and human history of the area. It can be obtained at the visitor center.

MORE THAN THE CAVE

The road slowly climbs west along the crest of the mountains past a large water tank and a pipeline—the park's water supply. Views extend south over the valley far below and north over the Walnut Canyon watershed. Mule deer and other desert animals are commonly seen, especially in the early morning and evening. After several miles, the road begins its descent into Walnut Canyon. Partway down, a small parking area marks the start of the Rattlesnake Canyon trail. It descends into the deep, rugged canyon visible just to the west. Desert rats will love the hike into the remote and little-visited canyon in the Carlsbad Caverns Wilderness. Be sure to take topographic maps and plenty of water. The trail is not well defined, and the country is dry.

As the road continues down into upper Walnut Canyon, it passes a few foundations and stone walls that mark the site of the old Lowe Ranch and spring. After the ranch site, the road winds down Walnut Canyon. Several side canyons invite exploration. Finally, the drive ends at the main highway at the base of the Big Hill.

If you are visiting in summer and if by now it's late afternoon, return to the visitor center and watch the evening bat flight at the natural entrance of the cave. Every summer evening as many as 300,000 bats fly from their cavern roost for a night of feeding on insects. During a heavy flight, the bats seem almost like smoke pouring from the cave entrance. A park ranger gives a talk at the amphitheater at the cave entrance before the somewhat unpredictable flights. As you watch the bats, enjoy the evening as the desert cools with the setting sun.

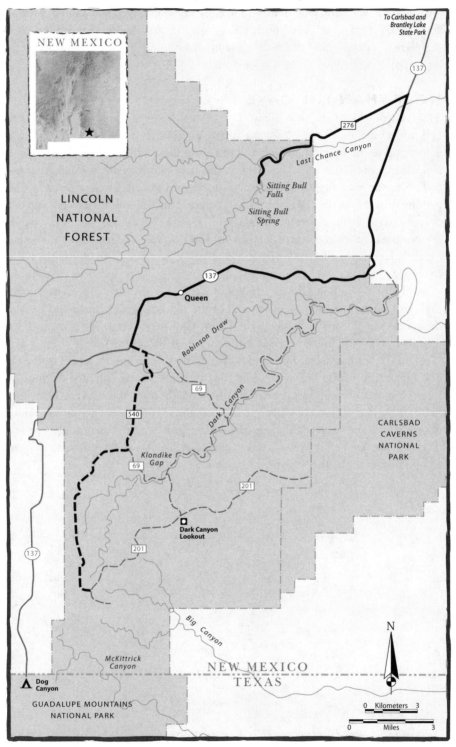

Sitting Bull Falls & the Ridge Road

SITTING BULL FALLS TO GUADALUPE RIDGE

GENERAL DESCRIPTION: A spectacular 38-mile paved and gravel route to a large spring-fed desert waterfall and the wooded high country of the Guadalupe Mountains.

SPECIAL ATTRACTIONS: Sitting Bull Falls, Guadalupe Mountains, Lincoln National Forest, ghost town of Queen, views, hiking, camping.

LOCATION: Southeastern New Mexico. The drive starts about 35 miles southwest of Carlsbad at the Sitting Bull Falls road junction along Highway 137.

DRIVE ROUTE NUMBER: Highway 137, Forest Roads 276 and 540.

TRAVEL SEASON: Year-round. The drive can be hot in summer but is most beautiful in late summer when rains turn the mountains green and increase the flow of Sitting Bull

Falls. The drive can be cold in winter but is usually reasonably pleasant. Snow is rare, but on occasion it can make the road slick and treacherous.

CAMPING: There are no formal campgrounds along the route, but the Lincoln National Forest allows primitive camping throughout most of the mountains. Nearby developed campgrounds lie at Dog Canyon in Guadalupe Mountains National Park near the end of the route and at Brantley Dam State Park near the start.

SERVICES: All services are available in nearby Carlsbad.

NEARBY ATTRACTIONS: Guadalupe Mountains National Park, Carlsbad Caverns National Park, Living Desert State Park, Brantley Dam State Park, President's Park.

THE DRIVE

In the hot desert foothills around Carlsbad, you don't expect to find a 100-foot waterfall. However, this drive leads to not only such a waterfall but also a streamside oasis and pine-covered mountains.

From Carlsbad, take U.S. Highway 285 north about 10 or 12 miles to the junction with Highway 137 near Brantley Dam. Follow paved Highway 137 about 24 miles to a paved road fork. The drive starts at the fork. Go right on FR 276 and follow the sign to **Sitting Bull Falls.** The road crosses the desert valley for a short distance before entering Last Chance Canyon at the boundary of the Lincoln National Forest. The canyon walls rise steeply, towering over the canyon bottom. Initially, desert vegetation predominates in the dry canyon. After a couple of miles, however, a few trees begin to appear in the canyon bottom, and a flowing stream usually appears about the time you pass a large side canyon.

The road ends in a large parking area with restrooms and picnic sites. There is drinking water here, but it tastes lousy. Remember to bring your own. On summer weekends, the falls and creek are popular escapes for area residents. The falls aren't visible from the parking area, and trees and sawgrass along the creek look out of place in the rugged desert canyon.

A short paved trail leads up the canyon and around a bend to the falls. Water cascades off the lip of an overhanging cliff 100 feet above and tumbles down into an emerald pool at the bottom. On hot days, kids and plenty of adults are usually playing in the pool and the creek downstream. The water flows from a large spring a little more than a mile upstream.

LEGEND OF THE FALLS

The water is laden with calcium carbonate, which is deposited as travertine on boulders and tree trunks at the base of the falls. The falling water creates a moist environment that supports ponderosa pines, Texas madrones, velvet ashes, and other trees in the narrow canyon. Maidenhair ferns and moss thrive on rocks moistened by the waterfall's spray.

Local legend has it that Chief Sitting Bull and his warriors were chased to the waterfall by ranchers after stealing livestock. However, the Indian chief was in Canada at the time and most likely never visited the area.

To hike above the falls, return to the picnic area at the parking lot. Another trail switchbacks up the hillside behind the picnic area and crosses the hilltop to the creek. Deep pools of clear water are lined by sawgrass and shaded by trees. Go downstream to find the lip of the falls. Use great care on the slippery edge; people have fallen and died. Hike upstream along the trail past more pools to get to the spring.

Unlike most of the national forest, Sitting Bull Falls is a day-use area only, and at night a gate is closed. After you've explored the falls area, drive back out the canyon to the junction with Highway 137. Turn right and head south toward the mountains.

The paved road begins climbing soon. Appropriately, the first piñon pines appear at about the time you enter the national forest. The road winds its way higher into the mountains, eventually topping out on a relatively flat plateau wooded with piñon pine and alligator juniper. A marker with a propeller mounted on it marks the site of an old plane wreck. The road passes a stone chimney, one of the few remnants of the town of Queen. The small ranching settlement was founded in 1905. At one time it boasted a post office and had a stage line connecting it with Carlsbad. However, by the 1920s the town had dwindled away. Today, there is a church camp, a Forest Service facility, and a few homes in the area of the old townsite.

CANYONS TO VIEW

About 18 miles from the turnoff to Sitting Bull Falls is the well-marked junction with FR 540. Turn left on the excellent gravel road, following the signs to the Guadalupe Ridge Road, Dark Canyon, and other destinations. The road soon

Sitting Bull Falls cascade, Lincoln National Forest

crosses Robinson Draw, notable for the large ponderosa pines in the bottom. The road climbs steadily south from the draw for about 3 miles to a road junction at Klondike Gap. The left-hand fork drops down into **Dark Canyon,** one of the Guadalupe Mountains' largest drainages and notorious for having flooded Carlsbad more than once. The roads along Dark Canyon and up to Dark Canyon Lookout are scenic, but road conditions are very changeable. Usually high-clearance or even four-wheel drive is necessary, especially on the road up to the lookout.

As you gain altitude, ponderosa pines become more common. In only 2 or 3 miles, FR 540 suddenly pops out on the west rim of the Guadalupe Mountains. The sheer escarpment falls as much as 1,400 feet down to the broad, grassy valley of **Dog Canyon.** The road hugs the brink of the escarpment for several miles, encouraging careful driving. A number of named vistas, some with interpretive signs, invite pauses in the drive. Beyond Dog Canyon and foothills of the Guadalupes, the Brokeoff Mountains, lie the Cornudas and Hueco Mountains near El Paso. To the northwest, the abrupt **Guadalupe Mountains** escarpment continues for many miles. Few people visit the rugged, isolated ridge. The Sacramento Mountains lie beyond the long ridge to the northwest. On a clear day, 12,003-foot Sierra Blanca Peak and the steel-blue outline of the Capitan Mountains are visible. Both lie more than 100 air miles away.

Shortly before the end of the drive, the road leaves the rim. The drive ends in a gravel parking area, although two unimproved roads continue on into the forest. The road to the left is usually in bad shape. The road to the right can usually be negotiated with great care by most vehicles. It climbs another 1.5 miles into the mountains before ending at an unsuccessful oil drilling location. A very bad road on the right, after 0.3 mile, leads to a spectacular overlook of North McKittrick Canyon and the high country of Guadalupe Mountains National Park. I suggest that you hike the easy 1-mile route to the canyon rim, rather than risking your vehicle. A left-hand fork at 1.1 miles goes out to a spectacular overlook of Big Canyon. Again, I suggest that you hike this bad side road rather than drive it.

This is one of the most heavily wooded areas of the Guadalupe Mountains. Ponderosa pine, piñon pine, and alligator juniper dominate the forest here. Most of the trees are not very tall because of the dry climate and frequent heavy winds. On moister north slopes, Douglas fir is relatively common. The Guadalupes are not high enough to support the lush forests of many other New Mexico mountain ranges; however, they still beat the desert heat far below.

Unfortunately, an arsonist started a forest fire here on a windy day in the very dry spring of 1990. The Guadalupes are notorious for their strong, prolonged winds. The fire was carried for miles through the Lincoln National Forest and all the way into Carlsbad Caverns National Park. When the ashes finally cooled, almost 30,000 acres of the most wooded part of the Guadalupe Mountains in New Mexico had been charred. The burned areas will probably eventually recover, but very slowly in the dry climate of these mountains.

31

The Black Range

MIMBRES VALLEY TO CHLORIDE

GENERAL DESCRIPTION: A 90-mile gravel and paved drive along the slopes of the Black Range, by two enormous wilderness areas, and ending at two former ghost towns.

SPECIAL ATTRACTIONS: Gila National Forest, Gila Wilderness, Aldo Leopold Wilderness, former ghost towns of Winston and Chloride, hiking, camping, scenic views.

LOCATION: Southwestern New Mexico. The drive starts at the north end of the Mimbres Valley about 35 miles northeast of Silver City.

DRIVE ROUTE NAME/NUMBER: Forest Road 150, Highway 59, Highway 52, county road.

TRAVEL SEASON: Year-round. Heavy rains in late summer or snows in winter can sometimes make the road impassable, especially FR 150.

CAMPING: The Forest Service maintains three small campgrounds along FR 150.

SERVICES: A store with gas is in Winston. The Mimbres Valley has food and gas. All services are in Silver City and Truth or Consequences.

NEARBY ATTRACTIONS: Gila Cliff Dwellings National Monument, City of Rocks State Park, Santa Rita open pit mine.

THE DRIVE

This drive crosses some of the most remote mountain country in New Mexico. Much of the drive follows a narrow corridor between the Gila Wilderness, the largest wilderness in the southwestern United States, and the Aldo Leopold, another sizable wilderness. The drive is ideal for those seeking solitude, outdoor activities, and classic southwestern mountain country. It travels north through the western slopes of the Black Range, cuts over the north end of the range, and curves back south to two small former mining towns in the eastern foothills. The Black Range is a long north–south, heavily forested mountain range with peaks that top out at more than 10,000 feet. The drive can be particularly beautiful in late summer after the rains have turned the forest and meadows lush and green.

The Forest Service recommends a high-clearance vehicle to do the part of this drive that follows FR 150 between its start at Highway 35 and Highway 59. The gravel road crosses steep, rugged country with many wash crossings that tend to get rough after rains. It can sometimes be done with a sedan after it has been graded during dry spells, but it is much easier and safer with a truck. The rest of the drive follows paved roads.

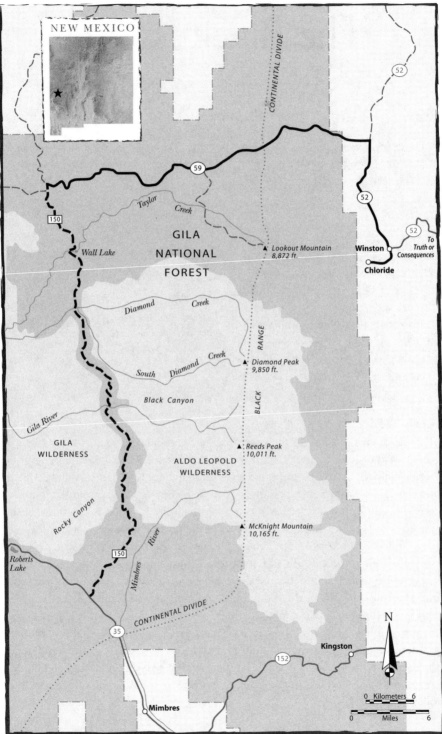

NEW MEXICO

CONTINENTAL DIVIDE

52

59

52

150

Taylor Creek

GILA

NATIONAL

FOREST

Wall Lake

▲ Lookout Mountain
8,872 ft.

Winston

52

To
Truth or
Consequences

Chloride

Diamond Creek

RANGE

South Diamond Creek

▲ Diamond Peak
9,850 ft.

Black Canyon

BLACK

Gila River

GILA
WILDERNESS

ALDO LEOPOLD
WILDERNESS

▲ Reeds Peak
10,011 ft.

Rocky Canyon

Mimbres River

150

▲ McKnight Mountain
10,165 ft.

Roberts
Lake

CONTINENTAL DIVIDE

35

152

Kingston

N

Mimbres

0 Kilometers 6

0 Miles 6

This drive begins along Highway 35 about 15.3 miles north of its junction with Highway 152 in the **Mimbres Valley.** The gravel road starts at about 6,500 feet in piñon-juniper forest. It climbs north onto **North Star Mesa,** roughly following the Continental Divide for several miles. Drainages to the east flow into the Atlantic; those to the west into the Pacific. If you have any doubts about the remoteness of the country you are about to enter, read the highway sign at the start that warns NO FOOD LODGING OR GASOLINE NEXT 120 MILES. Although at this writing there is gas and a small store in Winston about 90 miles away, it is best to start with a full tank and plenty of food and water.

North Star Mesa is a broad, gently sloping plateau between the Mimbres River and drainages that join the Gila River. Scattered piñon and alligator juniper trees dot the mesa top. Views stretch for miles. The road creates a corridor between the 558,000-acre **Gila Wilderness** to the west and the 202,000-acre **Aldo Leopold Wilderness** of the Black Range to the east. The two wildernesses were once one large wilderness area created in 1924 through the efforts of Aldo Leopold. He was greatly dismayed when this road was built, splitting it into two parts.

INTO THE WILDERNESS

Numerous trailheads lie along FR 150 marking routes into the Gila and Aldo Leopold Wildernesses. The Gila National Forest map and the two wilderness maps are very useful for this drive, especially if you plan to hike. They can be purchased at the forest ranger station a short distance south along Highway 35 from the start of this drive.

At 7.2 miles into the drive, Forest Road 150A splits off to the right, dropping down a short distance into the beautiful riparian corridor of the Mimbres River. Just half a mile past the turnoff is the Mimbres River and Continental Divide Trail trailhead on the right. Both are outstanding trails. One drops down to the Mimbres River and follows it for miles upstream through lush forest into its headwaters and ultimately the crest of the Black Range. The Continental Divide Trail climbs to the rugged crest of the range and follows it north. Ultimately you can follow the still-primitive route all the way along the Divide to the Canadian border.

Soon the road drops into a small canyon, the first of many that this drive will cross. Some tall ponderosa pines appear. The road descends into Rocky Canyon 11.5 miles into the drive. A forest of ponderosas, Douglas firs, and even a few aspens blanket the scenic, narrow, winding canyon. If there has been enough rain, there will sometimes be water flowing in the creek bottom. This stretch of the drive will often have the roughest road surface. A trail heads down Rocky Canyon into the Gila Wilderness from the small campground. Brannon Park is a nice day hike from the campground. The road climbs back up out of the canyon, reaching the trailhead for Trail 76 about 2 miles from the campground. The trail climbs high up into the Black Range, connecting with the Continental Divide Trail and other paths.

In another 2 miles the road passes the Trail 754 trailhead on the right in some beautiful ponderosa pine woodland. A pretty meadow with an old wooden fence lies on the right half a mile past the trailhead. In another mile or so, the road descends back into more dry piñon-juniper woodland and then into **Black Canyon.** Some interpretive signs and a turnoff to the two small Black Canyon campgrounds are on the left just before the bridge over the permanent creek. Just over the bridge is another turnoff on the right that goes a short distance up the canyon before ending at another trailhead at the Aldo Leopold Wilderness boundary. The trail follows the stream miles upstream and ultimately reaches the mountain crest near 10,011-foot Reeds Peak. Beaver and a rare native trout live in the creek's waters.

The road climbs right back out of Black Canyon, reaching Trail 716 on the left in about 2 miles. It and Trail 708 about 1.5 miles farther along can be used to hike across the Gila Wilderness to Gila Hot Springs and Gila Cliff Dwellings. An airstrip lies on the right about a mile past Trail 708. The road drops into South Diamond Creek 6.4 miles past the airstrip. In 1.3 miles the road reaches the confluence of South Diamond and Diamond Creek. Usually there isn't a permanent stream at the road crossing, but both canyons have permanent water upstream. Trail 68 follows South Diamond Creek far up into the Black Range while Trail 40 does the same up Diamond Creek from the end of a short spur road off FR 150.

In 5 miles the road passes **Wall Lake,** a small water body that is privately owned. It's fed by permanent Taylor Creek. There used to be a campground here but not any longer. The road surface improves a bit after the lake as it climbs up out of the canyon. There are some good views and more ponderosa pines. FR 150 meets Highway 59 about 7 miles past the lake in a big grassy valley. Go right on Highway 59. In 0.6 mile go right again at another junction, staying on Highway 59. The road is now paved! The Forest Service's Beaverhead work camp is a short distance to the left from the second junction.

The road steadily climbs east up over the north end of the Black Range through lots of ponderosa pine. Much of the area has had prescribed burns done in recent years to protect the forest from catastrophic fires. It creates a more open, parklike forest where most of the bigger trees can survive fires. The highway passes the Lookout Mountain turnoff on the right 16.5 miles after the beginning of pavement. It climbs up to a peak with a fire lookout and also goes to other destinations. The highway then passes a large meadow, Burnt Cabin Flat, right after the junction and then a restroom about a mile past the junction. Right after that the road crosses the Continental Divide at 7,670 feet and begins its descent down the eastern slopes of the mountains. You'll soon see a ranch and a power line on the right, the first significant signs of civilization since leaving the Mimbres Valley 65 miles earlier. The road passes through a small area of cabins in a private inholding. The forest turns slowly into piñon-juniper woodland and then into grassland with great views of the San Mateo Mountains to the northeast and the Black Range to the south.

Canoe at Wall Lake

WINSTON AND CHLORIDE

The highway reaches a restroom and interpretive sign at the national forest boundary 75 miles into the drive. In 2.5 miles Highway 59 ends at a junction with Highway 52. Turn right and follow Highway 52 south about 9 miles to the small village of **Winston.** It and its neighbor, **Chloride,** are two small mining towns that boomed from silver strikes in the 1880s. Like many small mining towns in the West, the boom ended in a few years, most mines closed in the 1890s, and the towns almost died. In recent years the ghost towns have come back to life but are still tiny. In their very remote location, they may never reach their population peaks of about 500 people each in the 1880s.

A small store offers drinks, gas, and snacks in Winston. To continue the drive to its end in Chloride, drive south through Winston on a county road past some old buildings and then some scattered trailers. Chloride lies over the hill about 2 miles from Winston in a canyon. A number of photogenic old buildings line the main street of the tiny village. It's hard to imagine that the town once had eight saloons, three general stores, three restaurants, a post office, and many other businesses. Today the few residents enjoy a quiet life far from the big city. From here the quickest way to get to Truth or Consequences, Silver City, or other destinations is to continue on Highway 52 to Interstate 25 in the Rio Grande Valley about 31 miles from Winston.

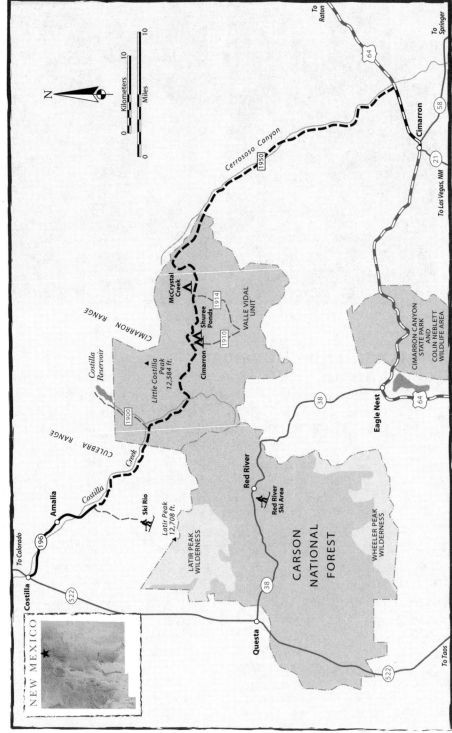

Valle Vidal

COSTILLA TO CIMARRON

GENERAL DESCRIPTION: A 69-mile drive through the high meadows and forests of the Sangre de Cristo Mountains.

SPECIAL ATTRACTIONS: Carson National Forest–Valle Vidal Unit, Sangre de Cristo Mountains, views, fall color, hiking, camping, fishing.

LOCATION: Northern New Mexico. The drive starts in Costilla at the junction of Highways 522 and 196 just south of the Colorado border.

DRIVE ROUTE NUMBER: Highway 196, Forest Road 1950, U.S. Highway 64.

TRAVEL SEASON: Late spring through fall. Snows close the higher parts of the road in winter. Late summer and fall are the most beautiful times of year.

CAMPING: The Forest Service maintains Cimarron and McCrystal Creek campgrounds. The privately owned Rio Costilla Park offers camping along Costilla Creek.

SERVICES: All services are available in Cimarron and nearby Questa. Costilla has gas and a restaurant.

NEARBY ATTRACTIONS: Taos Ski Valley, Rio Grande Gorge, Latir Lakes, Cimarron River Canyon.

THE DRIVE

Unlike much of the Sangre de Cristo Mountains around Taos and Santa Fe, this part of the range is lightly visited even though it's just as beautiful. The mountains are New Mexico's highest, with peaks exceeding 13,000 feet in elevation. The range is an extension of the Rocky Mountains of Colorado. This drive crosses the northernmost part of the Sangre de Cristos that lies within New Mexico. It passes by crystal-clear trout streams, a rugged gorge, high peaks, and vast meadows dotted with groves of aspen.

The drive starts in the village of **Costilla,** just south of the Colorado border. The small town lies at about 7,700 feet elevation, where the high sagebrush plains butt up against the mountains. Follow Highway 196 southeast through the village. If you want to camp in Rio Costilla Park or go up to the Latir Lakes, be sure to stop at the park (RCCLA) office on the right in town for information and permits. The road quickly leaves the small village and the high plains and enters a canyon with Costilla Creek gurgling down the bottom. Piñon pine and juniper cloak the hillsides. The canyon broadens into a valley at the settlement of Amalia after about 5 miles. Scattered homes and hay fields cover the valley floor. At about 8 miles the route passes the turnoff to Ski Rio on the right. The side road climbs 3.5 miles up to the ski area base. When it's open, the ski area has a great vertical drop, small lift lines, and more snow than most New Mexico resorts. However, drought and remoteness have affected the ski resort's profitability. At the time of this writing, the resort is closed.

HIGH PEAKS

After the Ski Rio turnoff, the road narrows but remains paved. It continues up the valley, passing scattered homes. Cottonwoods line the creek, and tall conifers begin to appear on the north-facing slopes of the valley. In 2.5 miles, the pavement ends at the boundary of **Rio Costilla Park,** and the valley soon narrows abruptly into a rugged canyon. The Culebra Range, part of the Sangre de Cristo Mountains, towers above, reaching almost 13,000 feet. Snow caps the highest peaks well into the summer. Just to the north, in Colorado, the range tops out at more than 14,000 feet. If the state line were a few miles north, New Mexico would have a 14,000-foot peak. The good gravel road winds through the deep gorge, pinched between the creek and the sheer rock walls that tower above. Fly fishermen test their skills in the clear creek waters. With a permit, you can camp and fish along the creek. The entrance to the **Latir Lakes** part of Rio Costilla Park is on the right about 4 miles after the end of pavement. The lakes are a cluster of small but scenic natural lakes formed by ancient glaciers. They lie high in the mountains at the foot of Latir Peak. Be sure to pick up a permit in Costilla if you want to go there. The park recommends a high-clearance four-wheel-drive vehicle to get to the lakes.

From the Latir Lakes turnoff, the drive continues up Costilla Creek for 2.3 more miles to the **Carson National Forest** boundary. The road becomes FR 1950. This section of the Carson National Forest is known as the Valle Vidal Unit. The 100,000-acre tract of high mountain terrain was once part of Vermejo Park Ranch, the huge adjoining ranch now owned by Ted Turner. It was donated to the people of America by Pennzoil in 1982 and became part of the Carson National Forest. The Forest Service manages Valle Vidal to enhance its wildlife potential. Off-road vehicle travel is not allowed. Particularly noteworthy is its large elk herd. The elk can often be seen on this drive, especially early and late in the day when they leave the forest and graze the meadows.

TO SHUREE PONDS

From the national forest boundary, the road continues up Costilla Creek for 1.5 miles to a road fork. The left fork follows Costilla Creek about 3 miles up to the forest boundary with private land. From the gate at the boundary, the dam for Costilla Reservoir can be seen. Continue the drive by staying right toward **Shuree Ponds** on FR 1950 at the fork. The road follows the much smaller Comanche Creek upstream through meadows and forested mountains that rise above. The small fenced exclosures along the valley bottom were built to study the effects of elk and livestock grazing on the creek. In a little more than 4 miles from the fork, the road begins to climb up out of the creek bottom. The views become tremendous as the road climbs up into broad meadows near 10,000 feet. Groves of aspen

Meadow at Valle Vidal, Carson National Forest

explode with color in fall along this stretch of road. Wheeler Peak, the highest point in New Mexico, and Baldy Mountain, another high peak, can be seen to the south across the vast meadows of Valle Vidal. After passing Clayton Corral in a mountain divide, the road descends to the turnoff to Cimarron Campground on the right. There is water at the campground. If you have a high-clearance vehicle and the weather is dry, you can follow Forest Roads 1910 and 1914 past the campground in a big loop that reconnects with FR 1950 some miles away.

From the campground turnoff, continue about another mile to Shuree Ponds, a series of ponds located in a beautiful meadow dotted with widely scattered ponderosa pines. There are picnic tables, a restroom, and an old lodge at the ponds. Be sure to stop and walk around the ponds. If you have a license, you can also try your luck with a fishing pole. One of the ponds is designated for children only. One trail leads half a mile to Cimarron Campground.

From Shuree Ponds the road climbs for a short distance to a divide. It then begins a long, winding descent out of the highest mountains to a lower area of ponderosa-pine–covered plateaus. Great views open up to the east and south. The loop road mentioned earlier rejoins FR 1950 on the right 4.3 miles from the ponds. The terrain levels out, and the road crosses big meadows and beautiful park-like groves of ponderosa pine. McCrystal Creek campground is on the left about 7 miles from the ponds.

TO CIMARRON

Beyond the campground, the terrain changes to high sandstone mesa country wooded with ponderosa. Some areas have been burned by recent forest fires. About 4 miles from the campground, the road begins a long, gradual descent down Lookout Canyon. At about the time the road leaves the national forest, Lookout Canyon joins Cerrososo Canyon and continues to follow it downstream. When the road leaves the Carson, it enters the private **Vermejo Park Ranch.** The ranch is part of the two-million-acre Maxwell Land Grant created in 1841. Ted Turner acquired it in 1996 and has been working to restore it to its original appearance. Cattle were removed and the range restocked with bison. With natural fires suppressed, the forest had become overly thick, so selective logging is being done to restore it to its natural state. The 588,000-acre ranch is still operated as a luxurious guest ranch for hunting, fishing, and other outdoor activities. The rest of the drive to US 64 crosses the ranch. It's posted, so please don't trespass.

As the road descends Cerrososo Canyon, the ponderosa pines thin out, and piñon-juniper forest begins to dominate. The canyon deepens and gets quite dramatic about 15 miles downstream from the forest boundary. About 4 miles later, the canyon opens up quite abruptly onto the western edge of the Great Plains. The gravel road soon ends at US 64. Turn right and follow the highway about 5 miles to the end of the drive in **Cimarron.** As you go, look for the remnants of the small ghost town of **Colfax** on the right. Not much remains. A crumbling old passenger railroad car is probably the most noteworthy ruin. Cimarron has all visitor services. See Drive 33 for more details about the small town.

Cimarron Canyon

CIMARRON TO EAGLE NEST

GENERAL DESCRIPTION: A 23-mile drive through the deep canyon of the Cimarron River.

SPECIAL ATTRACTIONS: Colin Neblett Wildlife Area, Cimarron Canyon State Park, Philmont Scout Ranch, Eagle Nest Lake, hiking, camping, fishing, views.

LOCATION: Northern New Mexico. The drive begins in the small town of Cimarron.

DRIVE ROUTE NUMBER: U.S. Highway 64.

TRAVEL SEASON: All year. Summer and fall are probably the most pleasant times for the

trip. Although the road is plowed, snow can sometimes make the drive treacherous in winter.

CAMPING: The state park and wildlife area in the canyon has three campgrounds.

SERVICES: Cimarron and Eagle Nest have all services. Ute Park has gas, a store, and a very small motel.

NEARBY ATTRACTIONS: Historic Taos, Taos Pueblo, Fort Union National Monument, Angel Fire and Red River ski areas, Wheeler Peak Wilderness, Carson National Forest, ghost town of Elizabethtown.

THE DRIVE

This drive follows the Cimarron River upstream through the deep canyon it has cut through the Cimarron Range, the easternmost flank of the Sangre de Cristo Mountains. The Sangre de Cristo Mountains are a southern extension of the Rocky Mountains of Colorado. The mountains contain New Mexico's highest peaks, some reaching higher than 13,000 feet in elevation.

The drive starts in the small town of **Cimarron.** Today it's a quiet tourist town, but it was once a notoriously rowdy place. In 1841 the Beaubien and Miranda Land Grant was filed, marking the beginning of the town. Lucien Maxwell acquired the grant by inheritance and purchase, and the tract became known as the Maxwell Land Grant. Cimarron became the headquarters for the vast 1.7-million-acre spread. At one time it included the towns of Raton, Springer, Cimarron, and Elizabethtown and areas such as the Carson National Forest's Valle Vidal Unit, Vermejo Park Ranch, Philmont Scout Ranch, and even parts of southern Colorado. Maxwell's massive house in Cimarron contained a gambling den, dance hall, billiard room, hotel, and even a whorehouse. The town became a principal stop on the Santa Fe Trail. Saloons and the like thrived, leading to numerous violent incidents at Maxwell's place and throughout the town. Notables such as Kit Carson, Buffalo Bill Cody, Zane Grey, Frederic Remington, and Davy Crockett passed through the town.

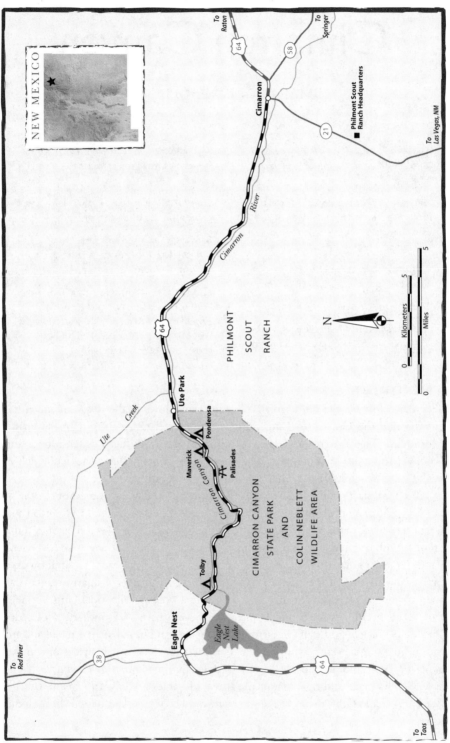

The St. James Hotel was built across the way from the Maxwell House and managed by Henry Lambert, a former chef for President Abraham Lincoln and General Ulysses S. Grant. The inn became popular with outlaws, including Clay Allison and Jesse James. Killings were common. The Las Vegas newspaper once wrote, "Everything is quiet in Cimarron. Nobody has been killed for three days."

Be sure to stop at the old downtown on the north side of US 64. There are several gift shops and similar tourist-oriented places to see. Less obvious, but even more interesting, is the other section of town across the river on Highway 21. This part of Cimarron is the site of Maxwell's house, the restored St. James Hotel, and the Old Mill Museum at Maxwell's Aztec Mill. Be sure to look at the original pressed-tin ceiling in the hotel dining room, once its saloon. Many bullet holes still remain.

After spending time in Cimarron, consider a short side trip south on Highway 21 before beginning the drive. The headquarters of the massive **Philmont Scout Ranch** lies only 4 miles south of town. A massive mansion was built by Tulsa oilman Waite Phillips in 1926 as headquarters for the ranch. The ranch was part of the Maxwell Land Grant and includes Kit Carson's old ranch. In 1938 Phillips donated part of the ranch to the Boy Scouts. The headquarters area includes the elegant old Phillips mansion, dining halls, housing, administrative offices, and a sea of tents, all sprawled across a beautiful site at the foot of the Sangre de Cristo Mountains. Today the ranch covers about 137,000 acres and an elevation range from about 6,500 to 12,441 feet. A scouting museum along the road tells the full story of the ranch.

Start the drive by heading west from Cimarron on US 64, following the Cimarron River upstream into the mountains. The Great Plains end here and the Rocky Mountains begin. The Cimarron Valley soon narrows into a canyon. The highway enters part of the Philmont Scout Ranch at 3.4 miles. High walls of sandstone rise on the north side of the canyon. Initially piñon-juniper forest cloaks the slopes; ponderosa pine, willow, and cottonwood thrive along the river. As you climb west, ponderosa pine becomes predominant on the slopes. At about 10 miles, the highway leaves Philmont, and the canyon opens into a broad valley known as Ute Park. The pretty valley contains a small mountain village. Baldy Mountain reaches high above the timberline on the northwest side of the valley.

In 2.5 miles the valley abruptly narrows back down into a deep canyon. The road enters **Cimarron Canyon State Park,** part of the **Colin Neblett Wildlife Area,** almost immediately. The road winds its way up the deep, wooded canyon. The state park offers fishing, hiking, camping, and even rock climbing on the high crags that tower over the canyon. Two campgrounds lie along the road less than a mile after entering the park. Be sure to stop on the right about 2 miles after entering the park in the narrowest part of the canyon. Towering cliffs of the Palisades Sill rise above the river on the right. The sill is a forty-million-year-old deposit of igneous monzonite that has been cut by the river. The elevation here is about 8,000 feet. Watch out for poison ivy on the river banks. There is no shortage.

Eagle Nest Lake

The road passes Tolby Campground on the right about 5 miles after the Palisades Sill. Look for beaver dams around the campground. Right after the campground, the highway climbs up out of the canyon to get around Eagle Nest Dam. In about a mile the road reaches a high point with great views of the Moreno Valley, Eagle Nest Lake, and the high peaks above Taos. **Eagle Nest Lake** was built by private interests in 1919 to store irrigation water for a farming area about 50 miles east. The lake lies at 8,218 feet and holds about 78,800 acre-feet of water. It is noted for its trout fishing. The high-altitude Moreno Valley, within which lie the lake and town of Eagle Nest, gets very cold in winter because cold air sinks into the valley and gets trapped. The drive ends in the town of Eagle Nest at the junction of US 64 and Highway 38.

Suggested Reading

Christiansen, Paige W. *The Story of Mining in New Mexico*. New Mexico Bureau of Mines and Mineral Resources, Socorro, NM, 1974.

Chronic, Halka. *Roadside Geology of New Mexico*. Mountain Press Publishing, Missoula, MT, 1987.

Fugate, Francis L. and Roberta B. *Roadside History of New Mexico*. Mountain Press Publishing, Missoula, MT, 1989.

Harbert, Nancy. *New Mexico*. Fifth edition. Compass American Guides, Fodor's, New York, 2004.

Parent, Laurence. *Hiking New Mexico*. The Globe Pequot Press, Guilford, CT, 1998.

Helpful Organizations

CHAMBERS OF COMMERCE, CONVENTION AND VISITOR BUREAUS, DEPARTMENTS OF TOURISM

Alamogordo Chamber of Commerce, 1301 North White Sands Boulevard, Alamogordo, NM 88310, (505) 437–6120

Albuquerque Convention and Visitor Bureau, P.O. Box 26866, Albuquerque, NM 87125, (505) 842–9918 or (800) 284–2282

Angel Fire Chamber of Commerce, P.O. Box 547, Angel Fire, NM 87710, (505) 377–6661 or (800) 446–8117

Carlsbad Convention and Visitor Bureau, P.O. Box 910, Carlsbad, NM 88220, (505) 887–6516 or (800) 221–1224

Chama Chamber of Commerce, P.O. Box 306, Chama, NM 87520, (505) 756–2306 or (800) 477–0149

Cimarron Chamber of Commerce, P.O. Box 604, Cimarron, NM 87714, (505) 376–2417 or (888) 376–2417

Cloudcroft Chamber of Commerce, P.O. Box 1290, Cloudcroft, NM 88317, (505) 682–2733

Eagle Nest Chamber of Commerce, P.O. Box 322, Eagle Nest, NM 87718, (505) 377–2420

Farmington Convention and Visitor Bureau, 3041 East Main Street, Farmington, NM 87402, (505) 326–7602 or (800) 448–1240

Grants Chamber of Commerce, P.O. Box 297, Grants, NM 87020, (505) 287–4802 or (800) 748–2142

Los Alamos/White Rock Chamber of Commerce, P.O. Box 460, Los Alamos, NM 87544, (505) 662–8105

Raton Chamber of Commerce, 100 Clayton Road, Raton, NM 87740, (505) 445–3689 or (800) 638–6161

Red River Chamber of Commerce, P.O. Box 870, Red River, NM 87558, (505) 754–2366 or (800) 348–6444

Ruidoso Chamber of Commerce, P.O. Box 698, Ruidoso, NM 88355, (505) 257–7395 or (800) 253–2255

Santa Fe Convention and Visitor Bureau, P.O. Box 909, Santa Fe, NM 87504-0909, (505) 955–6200 or (800) 777–2489

Silver City Chamber of Commerce, 201 North Hudson, Silver City, NM 88061, (505) 538–3785 or (800) 548–9378

Socorro Chamber of Commerce, P.O. Box 743, Socorro, NM 87801, (505) 835–0424

Taos Chamber of Commerce, P.O. Drawer I, Taos, NM 87571, (505) 758–3873 or (800) 732–8267

NATIONAL FORESTS

Carson National Forest, 208 Cruz Alta, Taos, NM 87571, (505) 758–6200

Carson National Forest, P.O. Box 68, Peñasco, NM 87553, (505) 587–2255

Carson National Forest, P.O. Box 110, Questa, NM 87556, (505) 586–0520

Carson National Forest, P.O. Box 469, Canjilon, NM 87515, (505) 684–2489

Carson National Forest, Tres Piedras Ranger District, P.O. Box 38, Tres Piedras, NM 87577, (505) 758–8678

Cibola National Forest, 1800 Lobo Canyon Road, Grants, NM 87020, (505) 287–8833

Cibola National Forest, 11776 Highway 337, Tijeras, NM 87059, (505) 281–3304

Cibola National Forest, P.O. Box 45, Magdalena, NM 87825, (505) 854–2381

Cibola National Forest, P.O. Box 69, Mountainair, NM 87036, (505) 847–2990

Gila National Forest, 3005 Camino Del Bosque, Silver City, NM 88061, (505) 388–8201

Gila National Forest, HC 68, Box 50, Mimbres, NM 88049, (505) 536–2250

Gila National Forest, P.O. Box 170, Reserve, NM 87830, (505) 533–6231

Gila National Forest, P.O. Box 8, Glenwood, NM 88039, (505) 539–2481

Lincoln National Forest, 901 Mechem Drive, Ruidoso, NM 88345, (505) 257–4095

Lincoln National Forest, Federal Building, Room 159, Carlsbad, NM 88220, (505) 885–4181

Lincoln National Forest, P.O. Box 288, Cloudcroft, NM 88317, (505) 682–2551

Rio Grande National Forest, 15571 County Road T5, La Jara, CO 81140, (719) 274–5193

Santa Fe National Forest, P.O. Box 150, Jemez Springs, NM 87025, (505) 829–3535

Santa Fe National Forest, P.O. Drawer 429, Pecos, NM (505) 757–6121

Santa Fe National Forest, 1474 Rodeo Road, Santa Fe, NM 87505, (505) 438–7840

NATIONAL MONUMENTS AND PARKS

Bandelier National Monument, HCR 1, Box 1, Suite 15, Los Alamos, NM 87544, (505) 672–3861

Capulin Volcano National Monument, P.O. Box 40, Capulin, NM 88414, (505) 278–2201

Carlsbad Cavern National Park, 3225 National Parks Highway, Carlsbad, NM 88220, (505) 785–2232

Chaco Culture National Historical Park, P.O. Box 220, Nageezi, NM 87037, (505) 786–7014

El Malpais National Monument, 123 East Roosevelt Avenue, Grants, NM 87020, (505) 783–4774

El Morro National Monument, HC 61, Box 43, Ramah, NM 87321, (505) 783–4226

Gila Cliff Dwellings National Monument, HC 68, Box 100, Silver City, NM 88061, (505) 536–9461

Pecos National Historical Park, P.O. Box 418, Pecos, NM 87552, (505) 757–6414

Salinas Pueblo Missions National Monument, P.O. Box 517, Mountainair, NM 87036, (505) 847–2585

White Sands National Monument, P.O. Box 1086, Holloman AFB, NM 88330, (505) 479–6124

NATIONAL RECREATION AND SCENIC AREAS

El Malpais National Conservation Area, Bureau of Land Management, P.O. Box 846, Grants, NM 87020, (505) 285–5406

OTHER ORGANIZATIONS

Cumbres and Toltec Scenic Railroad, P.O. Box 789, Chama, NM 87520, (505) 756–2151

Ghost Ranch Conference Center, HC 77, Box 11, Abiquiu, NM 87510-9601, (505) 685–4333

Turquoise Trail Association, P.O. Box 303, Sandia Park, NM 87047, (505) 281–5233

Index

About the Author

This is one of seven books of Laurence Parent's published by The Globe Pequot Press—the others are *Hiking Texas, Hiking New Mexico, Hiking Big Bend National Park, Scenic Driving Wyoming, Scenic Driving North Carolina,* and *Scenic Driving Texas.* He has also completed eighteen books for other publishers. His photos and articles appear in many national and regional magazines, calendars, and books. Recently he completed a small photo book on New Mexico and is working on large coffee table books on the Texas coast and black-and-white images of Texas.

Laurence was born and raised in New Mexico. After receiving a petroleum engineering degree at the University of Texas at Austin, he practiced engineering for six years before becoming a full-time freelance photographer and writer, specializing in landscape, travel, and nature subjects. He makes his home near Austin, Texas, with his wife Patricia and two children.

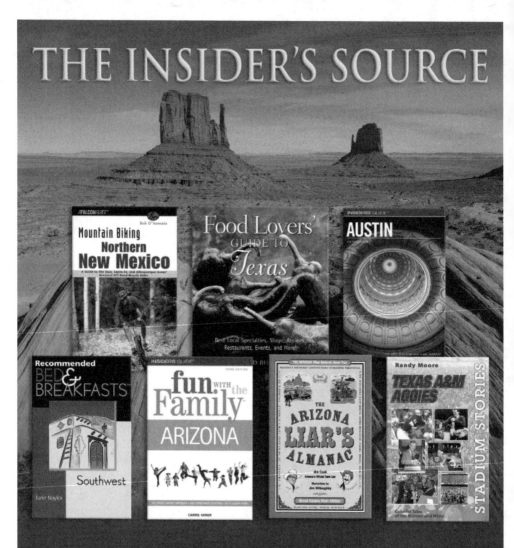